Backsliding

Backsliding

WritingElk Kelly

1 |

Chapter one

The Lord Wants to Bless You.

"The Lord Wants to Bless You, But..."

"Yeah? But what?"

"So, if that is true, why then is she a god, and not me?"

"God," they say, "wants to do this, and God wants to do that, but God can't do it because..." And he was like, "What! Why then is she a god and not me? Or you, or the other guy person over there without the shoe, on the feet, what is hindering them? What is that thing that is preventing your god, whom you say is all those things and can do all those things? What's preventing her from doing what she wants so very much to do? Like, to bless the brother, or the sister, for instance, and you? If she's a god, in truth, and if she really wants to do that, like bless the brother. What's preventing her?" Oh yeah, I forgot. It's him, the brother, and you, and me. It is us, all of us, and she who is to be blamed because we are the ones who are found here preventing her from doing it, by constantly doing all these other things, with you in it. "Oh, sweet sheet!" That's it, yes, another of the things that we should not be doing ever, but are always found to be doing, all the time. Nobody can ever stop us from doing these wrong things, not even her. But how did we get here, to the wrongdoers' end of the city square? Well, as for him, the brother? Listen to him, he's got an answer for you.

It was some savage beast from a wilderness theme that had bitten the brother hard in the crust of his bloodstream. Oh, how he hollered, oh how the brother screamed. But no one was found worthy enough to reach out and save him, well, so it would have seemed. He had to cry out yet more, had to curse at them, just to stop himself from popping open like a door, blowing up, and bursting, kaboom. "Oh, the poor..." Could he find you doing the wrong thing, though, like, when upon his imminent return, if he should find you and me, like, drifting, drifting away? Like some of us have been seen doing these days, even while doing all those other things, in the same unholy ways. Like, while you were there, a-lean, lean, leaning? Leaning on the wrong side of everything? Of course, not you, only the other Ewe, as in him. Elkhan the elk is what I mean, as it is in this case of rice and beans. He alone could be found guilty of such; it's now on your face over the wash basin in the house, no? "No."

But then again, it finally clicked and popped open when he saw how they reacted in response to it, then, like a token. The new project, you know. How normal it had become for them, the not-normal conditions, as it was seen happening over on our hometown's end. It came about in nasty, lethal looks that could kill lesser mortals than he had by then become, like a legal crook. Those types of looks must have killed him many times before: that's why he never got around to living at all. Living his life like he'd wanted to, not just sliding down the waterfall like a bore. But look, he's back now, and he's going to live, even if it kills him, and you? They did try to kill him, yes, if only in his spirit and dreams. But he wasn't going down without a fight. For this cause, though, some will even dare to die, for that cause too, if it is found to be as worthy as you, no, not I. As for Elkhan the elk, he believes in the cause, well, well, of course, his cause. These very causes, right here, are included in there. Even though he knows very well that the long knives are already out, and are on the millstone, grinding. They're grinding away at it and sharpening it razor-sharp today, getting ready for the attack and the neck-slit, okay? "Yes."

Everybody was readying themselves for the slaughtering in the dark, king, and backflips. But. "Come along now," said he, "let's reason this out together."

They'd sanctioned a son, a member of the service, from free service to them, Sis, and for what? For daring to do something other than that, or this. You know! Like, something unthinkable to them. For daring to create something like a cap for his head-top — "No, stop."

"Okay." What kind of people do things like that anyway? Well, listen up, I'll tell you. The kind of people who have lost their way. They're not bad people, they're just lost people, yay. They might just need someone to redirect them and get them to refocus.

Elk would have gotten himself benched by the governing body of the church (the circus). "For four weeks," they'd said, like a curse. That would mean four weeks of him sitting down quietly and doing nothing in church, like me, you know. Well, not nothing-nothing. In reality, it was four weeks of him not serving in the church in his usual capacity as a musician. Sometimes, as a scripture reader to the pastor and other preachers who might be there on a mission, yay, it's a fun time; strike up the ignition. As the secretary and treasurer for the men's fellowship, and to a lesser extent, as a school bus driver for the Sunday school department, among other things that could fit in the yellow ship. To a lesser extent, in the case of the bus driver bit here, because had it been left up to the whims and fancies of the main instigator of these events' antics, Clair. He would still be there; vroom, vroom, vrooming around and beep, beep, beeping away at driving the church bus into space today.

This was to serve as a point to rally and get him to think very critically. In thinking, he'd managed to discover a few more "*sin Ting*" somethings amongst them. Like, he was to find out that: There are some jobs that everyone seemed willing, "Able?" "Perhaps not," and even delighted to do on any given day, even under the table. "Yea-you." Some not so much so, but still, I'd say. There won't be any trouble in finding takers for those same types of jobs. This leaves us with two other types to consider for the crabs: (a) the job that people may think that everybody, including you, and yes, me too. You really love it or should love to do that job, and you don't want to be prevented from doing it at all, right? And (b), then there's the one that no one else wants to do or was found capable of doing, one shoe in. In this case, that job is driving the Sunday school bus for them into space. Or even to take the rest of us into "our" comforts (for goodness' sake) in those days, and why? It's because it's way too demanding and time-consuming a job for them, my guy. On top of the fact that such a person has got to be very well-trained and certified at what she does in this wise. Quite unlike most, or all else, there among them, and their wives.

"Oh, Chru-ice!"

"Yes, just the words I heard him cry that night." So, the person who (for whatever reason) decides to take this on, it will be his job (or hers) for the long haul.

"Four weeks," they'd said, of him being benched, but then came the question from the other friendly gents as to what that meant? "What does it entail for him?"

"He should sit down and do nothing in the church; don't let him play the music or read the scripture for the pastor during Sunday morning worship service, as was the custom before this." That was the reply, like a curse.

"He also drives the bus," came a quick reminder from another who was sitting there amongst them and us. Then came the qualifications from, guess who, behind her bus stand? Yes, you, you've got it right, Mom. From the main instigator of the suspension actions in proper, ma-man, no less. He suddenly wanted to screen out that part of the youth's many jobs. Those that the Elk was found doing there for them, at the time, so that he would continue doing that thing (perhaps), since no one else was found able, or willing to do it. Again, we say, "perhaps," to these things, since we don't know, and will never know exactly what others think, on such to-do lists. "Oh!" "Very convenient," said the Elk that evening, to them and us, little miss. That was when and where the conversation took a dramatic turn, and has been spinning, spinning, spinning away ever since, on corners and turns. All along the winding road through the gully of ferns. "Why get angry, though?" asked the Elk on the way to go, especially when one can't even get "even." Not even a better bowing-out reason. "Get Insight," said the Elk that night, get insights instead.

Mere days after the fallout with the church leadership, because of that and this. The attitudes, rhetoric, and behavioral patterns of many among them who were there to sit suddenly began to change. Words, statements, and terms in their arguments that were never used in the past. (Not in our hearing, at least, since you'd asked).

These all started rolling off people's tongues. Even coming from the pulpit back home, and fast, to go and sit on somebody's old bones as... I mean, back to the task.

Take this from someone who would have been there for well over twenty years, sitting in a very prominent and somewhat privileged position of theirs. Somewhere nearer than you, to the chieftain's rock (King chair).

"Or was... wasn't it around the pulpit?"

"Oh sheet!" Yes, that was it, there. Gulp, now, sit. Close enough to have been able to see and hear quite a bit of theirs. But there was never any such rhetoric.

"There was no need for it," one might suppose to say so and spit. Everybody was sitting in their comfort zone under their noses and looking down on this. But then, what would have changed? How come one doesn't usually see those types of heavy-handed reactions falling on blame, like that one, as was to be seen when meted out to others, as it applies to misbehavior? "Oh, my savior!" Cried the old man. Misbehaviors such as these that are common amongst them and their friends, "Holey graveyard!" Someone probably got tired of seeing the deadness, woke up, and spoke up, I guess, and that was when...

Of course, they would have tried to pacify the situation, tried to fix it, as usual, mi bredda man. Or sweep it under the carpet for the school gal (de nedda wan), you know, and the other girls.

"Which, which girls, those from the Netherlands?"

"Yes. But this wasn't the usual this time." What they didn't know at the time was this: the person they were there trying to fix this time was the fixer of people who were trying to fix people and solve these crimes. He'd come with a mission to get some things fixed, miss, and "fix" he would, (or would not), depending on what some gods might think of the pruning fork. Even though he knows that sometimes, things have to get a whole lot worse before they get better, and boy, did they ever get worse? Yes, of course, mi bredda, they did. They sure did, and they are still getting worse today, my brother's man's kid.

"But why, though, why were they so badly shaken up?"

"Oh! Could it be that, like, because they've been 'shown up,' and were surely not happy about that cup of mannish water?"

Drink, shrink. Drink it up. Why were they so mad? Why are they still so very mad at the man, and for what? I mean, really? Why did they react in such a manner, Neily? Could it be because such things are not allowed in Christendom? Or is it just among them, and the sixth one's dumb...?

It could have been you know, or it could have been because they don't know the difference between fiction and facts. Or between fantasy and reality, odd things such as that, though, could never be. Or could it? Imagination is something to be crushed by them, so it would seem to me mi maaga fren, sorry, I meant to say, my meager friend. In their neck of the woods (dead pen) and their dreams. Well, this man right here, Elkhan the Elk. No, not the bear staking out the rear, but him.

He seems to us to be a wild-ass type of an Ishmael-ish, mail-ish type of male. He won't be tamed. Surely, won't be blamed, nor will he take any of those names that they may try to force upon him. Unless it's the one that he wants to be liked by. Like, "free," just for instance. Free to see, free to be, free to be what he wants Ted to be, I mean, wanted, and that thing that he wants most to be, as it would seem to you and me, is free. Period.

So, as it appeared to some, down there on the row. He threw them a baited plum, and they swallowed it down, hook, line, and sinker, round, and ran with it, on the go. How could they, even after the brother had been telling them for months, down the way? Well, I know how, of course, the Elk had been following foo L, I mean. The Elk had been following some people who didn't portray the attributes of the wise and prudent.

Therefore, it must have been the other types that he'd been following, like Prudence. We've all been following her, whether or not one wants to admit it, my pops, it was them. They are people like himself, his very own self sitting there on the shelf, yes, him and the neat wheats. That's the kind of people "leaders" that he had been following for weeks. Like... Like, against his will, to state the following: like, all this time. Well, there comes a time in everybody's life and mine, a time when we must all heed another kind of call down the pipelines. That time is now for this other kind of guy cow, and wow! "I won't get mad anymore," said the Elk to the back door near the plow. I'll just get insights now. Yes, I will get insights instead.

Suppose you were a kind of person who was industrious, though, and like, astute, and aware. Suppose one would have risen from amongst you? Yes, even from there. One who'd gotten a strange and weird idea that she could invent and create things? Things like: let's just say, writing books, for example, albeit, the one that stinks like a da... uh, never mind him. Then went out and wrote one (badly) and trampled it.

Suppose all that was needed to make that badly written book into a great book, and gladly so, was a good agent, a good editor, a good publisher, and a good marketer from these nooks? Suppose that was what the brother man and his sister were searching for, from amongst you, and the crooks? Suppose that sort could have been found coming from amongst you, and yeah, them too?

What if that was exactly what the brother and his sister were trying to find, coming from among you and your friends when he was there lying... uh, I mean, talking about it all those times, in the end? He (probably) would have wanted us as a people to reap and keep the benefits in the house, yeah, as much as the chorus. In the family, and on the family lines, too. What if you'd missed out on a grand opportunity here, and the wines, or even the beers, coming in kinds, from where? "Yes, there." What if it was all your fault? Like, your ineptitude, and you being so "Salt..." I mean, salty? But then again, we all do know the truth, that isn't the case here, my youth. Right, Gertrude, dear? So, Mutant Pinochet. No, not yet. Well, good night, death, go fret.

"Are you a Christian?" They were quick to ask about this around the fish pan. This roughly translates into meaning: do nothing with your life, except what I tell you to do tonight, perhaps, and only so far as I may allow you the rights. Because whatever you think that you can do, I can do that too, and better. You must never outshine, outperform, out nothing me. Ensure that you never do or be. Nor should you ever become anything, like her, so as not to show me up towards the stairways of heaven, to see, mi cous.

My kind of people, and I don't want to be shown up that way. Even if you think that it's the easiest way to stay. It's a sin to do so. But, as said before, the Elk is that kind of a wild ass of a man and a bore. So, here we go again, Clor.

Shouldn't one strive for change, though, like, for betterment? Shouldn't one at least try to change the way one does the things that such a one may do, for them even? The things that one does, period? After that, one should have found out that one had been fooled, for instance. Tricked too, by the weak ones, and made to sign away one's rights, on brick stands? "Woo, that was cute, a bit, man."

"I know, but, but..." Okay, how about one's life and one's freedom, or money, and that was before such a person had gotten to know that she has any. The money that is? Or even how much she was worth (a half penny) working on gigs? But they, the other "they, them," they knew it all along. Who do you think it was that had given you your Gods and the books of rules? Supervisory powers, too, and other such controlling tools? Then came their many demands for you to provide them with periodic reports, by way of the finger and pen. "Keep moving, gentlemen, all be merry and bright". Yeah! That's right.

Probably so designed as to keep a watchful eye on you, even in courted courts and courting the wives. To make sure that what you're doing within your walls over there, day and night, conforms to their plans for you and all, my dear? Tell me, who was he, or she, that person or good godly personality? Who was it that would have done all those things on the whole sum of us? It was him, yes, it was them.

Kiss mi teeth, though. What a whole heap of an allahbaloo when ebbrey baddy dun knoah sey nutton nuh goh soh. Much ado about nothing, because everyone already knows that that's not the way things usually work on the spin, go. Back now, though, to the point at hand, no? "Yes." After the brother was made aware of all these things. After getting a glimpse of where he was, and of all of the entities who (seemingly) had vested interest in keeping him enslaved, and fat. Are you feeling me? "Yes." Okay, I guess that...

But not as fat as in, free-flowing facts, nor cash, ignorant too, and in chains, to go serve them in perpetuity, again. Growing more into loving it every day, and watching his fortune and birthright slipping away.

Having found this out, though, and having gotten a glimpse into how far beyond the limits he was. Heading deeper in and into perpetuity on this, too, oh, yes, and the bugs. After finding out all this, and the benefits of a fur coat for the little miss, should such a person continue going along that same path unabated, and to the pits, as they did? Should he not begin to try and change some things, like, to try plugging the holes that were there draining him?

Shouldn't he try to set some priorities in his life? Shouldn't he start with the most logical and least costly things, then work his way in from there? In other words, what would Jeezas... I mean, Jesus, what would Jesus do to care, in a case such as this, here? If there was a God somewhere, and let's say, there was something that she wanted him to know, wouldn't she have written it down somewhere and framed it to stay that way, and get them to be able to show?

So that one, anyone at all... "Everyone, even." So that everyone might be able to find it and read it to become wise, too, as he did? Wouldn't she, Boo? Mi rathid! Wouldn't she say something like: give no sleep to your eyes, nor rest to your eyelids until you've delivered yourself out of their cribs of mischief? Or out of their hands, and break the yoke? Wouldn't she? Yes, she would, no joke. So, what now?

Do you now want the truth? What is truth? Where's your truth anyway? Can you handle the truth today? Well, here are some truths for your austerity measures, then. But don't shoot just yet, mi fren, wait on my friend, over there. At least, not before I'm done with them. I'm just the messenger here, you know, and the tray-carrier bringing in the rum and imported beers.

So, "What is the truth?" I again asked the youth. If one should run a Google search on the Earth, or consult a dictionary on the term, "What is truth?" One would be more than likely to find answers that describe the truth as (a) the quality or state of being true. (b) Truth conforms to reality. C, Truth is most often used to mean being in accordance with the facts or reality, or fidelity to the original standard. Among other things, such as the uglier pal amongst the vanguard.

Regarding how truth applies to this story, though, and regarding the Elk's view on this and some other things, to show it to the dorm guard. Let's try and see if we can say what the truth is to him, and I, as we sometimes get to see it in our visions, from within, the I... The Earth as it is now is the truth. In the sense that this mass of collective matter right here under our boots is here, even now, in its many and varied forms, it is here, somehow.

We as people inhabit her crust, and she sustains us in the bus... Ted's vehicle, for a while. A very short while in the grand scheme of earthly things to spoil the we-group, I'm in. Come to think of it, this, too, is the truth. After we've done our "short while" here, we will expire, beware. Quite unlike your bottled beer, which never retires. Another degree of truth, to hang on the wire, my youth, dear, well, maybe. Because one may argue that said life is finished on the day that such a one expires.

Others may argue that life never ends, it continues forever and ever, amen. One only transcends from one state of being to yet another state, or realm. Truth, or facts? Or perhaps it's just an argument of such? A convincing argument, even. But whatever the case may be, this evening. Even if one should conclude that this, too, is true, it may only amount to a version of the truth, or two. Even a diminished version of the truth, like you.

Here, then, are some more truths for you, as seen through the eyes of Elkhan the Elk, and another few. "I'm here," the Elk had said to the pair. Right now, as you're here reading this too, in bed, sipping beer, perhaps. Whatever the case, though, the Elk was here, and so... How much longer will he be here? That's as good a guess as there are people who make those wild guesses and gears, unless... "Unless what?"

Unless there really is some all-knowing, intelligent being somewhere out there in the Mourn Inns. Someone, or something, who knows, and who does understand these things, and cares about the causes, Hugo. "Yawning." One who, from time to time, may venture into manipulating those things one way or the other, to make sure that everything works out right for her brother. If she should then choose to share that information with some well-placed, chosen folks like... like your holy father. Folks who are likely to be found in some very special and highly privileged positions, or another. Then there may yet be some other truths to decipher here, too, as it applies to you and me, and to the way I see things going through these forests of ancient trees. Those very few things that folks such as you and I get a chance to see. They lie in me, finding out who I am, who I really am, and getting to find out the harsh results about some things that I might have done. Things that would have featured well too, in bringing about these current ventures into questioning truths and other such schemes of things, towards the outcomes.

How faithful is your god? How faithful are you to your god, and to your belief in her? (Or him, if you prefer the masculine term here, to spin). What did she say to you? What did she tell you, or ask of you, versus what you, me, all of us, like, we? All sitting idling here on the "may-reach" bus near the tree of his. Versus what we think it was that she'd said? Is that "something" we strongly believe to be the "done" thing that she had said? Was it what she'd, in reality, said? Ee mi bred, tell me nuh man! Was that what she'd said? Are those two things, both the same and one, all the time? Am I allowed to ask this one, or is it a crime?

Elk would have said it first in that meeting, yes, the one that was hastily called to sanction him, for writing a book, or some such other thing. A book that they weren't very pleased with because the contents were not to their liking, (sit, sit, yes). So, they had to straighten him out. Yes, folks, Elk had some things to say to them, too, there and then.
He wanted to tell them, and he would have gone straight ahead and told them. Among other things, he'd said, "Sometimes love has got to be cruel, to be kind." He wasn't about to stop there at the line either, not this time, meager. He was going to say it again. "Sometimes," he said. "Sometimes love has got to be cruel, mi bred, really cruel, to be kind to them. Learn that and be wise, my friends."
If you have an issue with him on this, in disguise, just remember the other bits' eyes. "Don't get mad," you might have heard them say. Get even, instead, or go away, yes, go to bed. But what good is there in either of those, getting mad, or getting "even," even a rose, to be glad, Miss Stevens? I'd say, in agreement with the Elk himself today. "Get insights, instead."
So, when he was tempted to get mad at those folks, for what at the time he had construed to be unjust and unreasonable treatment, of course, it

had begun to dawn on him that this here is yet another great occasion to be fair and garner some beer. Well, no, not that, but some really valuable insights from them, to hear. So, insights it's been, ever since, my dear.

Chapter two

Out of the Blue They Came.
We don't need her type of talent and skills, no. Not those "worldly" types, if you will, because those types can kill. What we do need are pastors, lots of those, so pastors it is, of course. They'd said that the brother was stingy and mean, too, which might have very well been the case with the shoe I leaned onto. There could have been a whole lot more than just that going on in the brother's life at the time, and behind the front door of mine. In your face, too, and the washbasin, no denying. Much more than what meets the eye, Hingh, yes, your eyes even. Fun and jokes aside, though, there could have been something else going on there with that fellow, like something that neither the brother nor the Lord would have bothered to tell us, them, or you about. For whatever reason, hence the closing of the mouth. They, too, with all of their in-depth hearing, seeing, and Saw, Hingh, never saw that one coming, nor saw it when it came in.

"Oh, such a shame, Hingh."

"Sure thing."

So, you thought that it was because the Elk was stingy, that's why he wasn't paying you any more tithes and offerings, right, Binghy? What, then, does that say about you and the offspring tonight, and what about the all-knowing gods and the bright? What in particular does it say about the all-knowing part of it (the whole thing), and like, about how she's always talking to you and telling you things? How come she never bothered to tell you that part of the story, which was the real stored-up sin?

...

Every once in a while, the unexpected happens, an anomaly or such. So, out of the blue, she came in with her husband and family and moved up. With them, too, came her children. Very talented, ultra-driven, able, and capable. Yes, a very capable individual she was, with a knock and drive for business, quite unlike me and the others in the church communities, and sitting comfortably on the boards. She joined up with them and quickly settled into each role she was given. (They quickly gave them to her, one after the other). An administrator role was a good call after all, no better person could be found among them for such a role, Call, no, none at all. She did that well. "Too well," some had said, which was to lead to yet other tasks being placed on her, and upon her head atop the Bred...

Yes, my brother. They must not let her escape, no matter what; they can't afford to lose such a person as this one. So, they're going to teach her those things that she must learn. After she's done with all that learning, they will have to teach her some more and train her, Kern.

Then they will have to make it appear as if it was all worth something, a no-brainer.

"Other than what was to be there on top of the cornmeal dumplings?"

"Yes, like, those beside the strainer, well, perhaps." So, they had to teach her some more, although none of them were teachers, I'm sure.

"Really?"

"Yes, really," and then, they gave her a title and a bible, and made her a pastor, too. Another pastor has now been added to the very many that are already there grazing in that pasture beside you.

"Phew!"

"True, that's what I did, too." Which was already too many for one tiny churchlette of a church, and too few pennies for the pauper, from the purse, and that was without regard to first verifying whether she was able, capable, or in any way cut out for that part of the pasture. But pastors are what these people are after. Because pastors are what they need most of all, sir, yes, go ask her, she should know. So, pastors are what they get, of course.

Meanwhile, whether or not it was because of those things, the effect was the same for the wearing and tearing of the poor thing. The sister-turned-pastor had probably gotten to the point where she'd found too many things on her plate eyeing her, and in her name to handle anymore. So much so that she couldn't bear them all at once to remain in their good grace and continue going on to the dance floor, Sister Grace; some things, therefore, would have to go. Yes, others have a way of coming to that self-same realization, I guess. Not just the brother who had to cut some things off on the financial side of the ledger, at his address. The sister-turned-pastor found herself having to shed loads, too. Then, the thriving business she'd started at first, which was the very reason why she caught their eye and their attention, to her curse, anew.

"True, true."

That said, business was soon to be no more, and twist it and call it something else as much as one may want to, as before, the effects of that were the same. The business was gone, and so too was the prospect of inspiring another one. Like, a young person from among them, let's say, to go out and start another business of their own, too, one day. In this business where... sorry, I meant to say, place, in this place where business is "the way to go." But we didn't know. What we wanted was churches, more than anything else in the world, kids. So, church it is, go figure. In the meantime, the brother was looking on, and...

Elkhan did contribute greatly to the plan and made himself out to be an outcast. Happened when he would have gotten the misguided, devil-inspired idea of writing a book and offering it for sale on the open market in Arcadia on the nook, so fast. It wasn't so much the writing of the book, though, as it would have seemed to Ayvia, below. Because he'd written other books before, and sold many amongst them, and more. There never was an issue with any of those, then. If there was, it would have been covert. But now, he has gone way too far out. How dare he, yes, him, to go and write a book about love and sex, not the king? Relationships in the car, too, and such, even more of it than the verses in the book — "And, and the chorus?" "Yes." Much more than that, too, were these on the way out. How dare he be so overt, brazen, and realistic, true to his plot and his characters' misfits? Too craven and lickerish, to go all the way and say things as they really are? How dare he, him? Trying to be good at what he does, and was still there, doing? To strive for excellence is what I mean. How dare he, yes, him, again? Can't have that sort of thing, my friend, not around here, not on these lot-tory pots; those beloved games of theirs. There have got to be some sanctions against him here. We've got to make an example out of him to go around and share, so that others may see, or hear of it, and beware. In the meantime, the brother was looking on and seeing some other things going on around him in signs, such as these.

...

Timothy and others have been moving on, getting out and up towards the prosperous rung. They've now joined up with Chetalee's foundation and are going all out, and about making inroads into black communities and black countries worldwide. But not that alone; they're going out recruiting other rich black folks, from the elite athletes, and down to you, and yeah! I know that includes me, too. Actors, entertainers, and down to the business, and "other" professional types of gainers. They have been getting on board with the initiative in droves. The result of these efforts has given rise to a brand-new era, a new way of thinking in the modern black population, where you are. Young blacks are rising and raising hell. Rising to the challenges, too, as you can tell. Focusing on education, skills training, career-building, and you. Business management training, too, and more things to do. Wherever in the world black folks are today, the current runs through the highway, and things are starting to happen for them and you. Well, not all of them, some are still going to Sunday school. The activities are now heated up to a fever pitch. Come, take a look at this. When Chetalee first got started on the journey, she didn't know anything, nor did we. She only knew enough to have known that she didn't know. As for the rest of us, as a whole, we too didn't seem to know what we all needed to know, to get to the next level, on the go, where we could become more than just the perpetual servant class, you know. At the time, too, we were glorying in it, seemingly. "Yes, it's true."

"I know, that's why I'm here now, telling the others who are standing by you." She had to establish an education fund, designed to fund promising young minds (promising young black minds only) through institutions of higher learning, and beyond, all around the gum tree. It was not easy; she would have lost quite a few of her most promising prospects along the way home to feed me, in the early days. But she had factored those possibilities into the mix from day one, as it says. She and her team just shook it off their heads and continued pressing forward and onward, mi bred. The result is now becoming clear for all to see, including the naysayers pounding it on the drywall like me. Graduates from these early initiatives can be found heading several nursery projects and startup institutions today, in the Caribbean, Africa, Asia, and further afield. Wherever black people were, and are, people who had finally woken up to the realization of where we as a people really were, in the grand and glorious scheme of things, on the floor. Such people were starting to realize that it was not good. Had come to realize, too, that that was never going to be good. They have now caught on to the vision of where we need to go and what we must do to get there. These folks are now eager to join in, ready and willing to put their shoulders to the wheel and steer, to get a move forward, well, so I hear. The foundation has been showing up there alongside them, wherever these people are in the world, and hiding. They are showing up armed and ready to assist and enable them. "Give people purpose, show them the possibilities, and anything can, and will happen," she had said, Chetalee it was, who was heard saying this.

...

If Chii did it, so can you, and yes, me too. Have you noticed the shift? Yes, some others from among the brothers have been taking notice. Imagine with me for a moment. Imagine how the Chinese are doing it these days. They're going throughout the developing world, such as Africa, the Caribbean, etc., lending money to them and building things such as roads. Railways and many other types of mega infrastructure to stay and spend on codes, okay?

They're masters of these sorts of things these days, yeah. But they didn't get to be that good overnight, no way. Don't be afraid of stage fright, I'd say. It probably took them years, decades, centuries, perhaps, to hone their skills and perfect the arts. Just imagine that Chinese engineer who just designed and built you that fine highway on the home end. He was once a baby, you know, just like you were, and I too, now we are all grown men, and maybe more so than them, yes. But he, too, grew up, and someone would have taught him how to design and build highways. That someone was most likely in his family lineage, doing things "My way." Let's say it was his great-grandfather who was the very first in the family to have ventured out and taken a shot at building roads off the highway. Probably just a stone pathway into his yard, using bricks, stones, or boards, all night, all day. But he did it well enough to have garnered some interest and admiring stares from passers-by and the guards over there, no less. Then the words started getting around,

"Have you seen Chii's walkway on the grounds? That thing sure looks good, boy." So, you know that every other Chinese man and his first cousin is now going to want an upgrade to his walkway too, and by the dozen, "Ooh! What a joy!" Chii is now starting to get path-building jobs and many more opportunities to practice and hone his skills. "Mi god!"

"Yes, but... just chill." Chii is surely going to get his hands and fingers bruised and battered in the process. But that will not hinder him from going on to progress. Chii then started looking at ways to make his job easier and the workload lighter. So, he brought in his sons; one, two, three. All of them were to come, and then comes the lady — "Yuh mean, she?"

"Yes, she went in too, when he invited his and hers to come and see them, yes, his daughters came and joined him too. Because the business is now booming anew, he even had to invest in some heavy-duty tools, then invent some more to pay off the debt he had to borrow to help him pay the fools." But as for you and me, what kind of people are we? We pray for jobs, always, instead of going out and creating them for ourselves and our children in the coming days. Keep praying for those jobs. The robots are coming and, as for them. They ain't praying none. So, what the heck can they do anyway? Absolutely nothing I'd say. Right?

"Right."

Chapter three

What Has God Done for You Lately?

What has God done for you in recent times? What more can she do for you, instead of crimes? What have you asked her to do for you lately? Did she do it hastily? Are you asking for the right things with her giving hands? Are we as a people asking the right things of her, Maman? Sure, you can consider it, so consider this one. Should one, somehow, find out that one usually gets what one asks for at hers, and you did ask, and found that you'd gotten the very things that you'd asked for, from the boss, even, as it occurs? How well is it working for you now? I mean, really? Things are working just fine for you now, right? So, what more could you, or should you, have asked for? What more should you be asking for, even now? Did you leave out something that was very important and should have featured in the asking? I'm just asking.

Suppose you should find out that you're on your own, though, or worse? What if you should find out that you're your own worst enemy? Of course, that's a farce, but what if it's not, both in the individual, as well as the collective sense of the term, to see the old-school general on the lot? Like, how did you, as an individual, and "us" as a people, get to such a place as this? How did we get this comfortable in our collective misery on our faces? How did you, how did we? Is this all that there is to life for people like us to be? Should we even ponder these questions, or ask a wife of him — "And me?"

"Probably." Did we as a people ever stop to think for a moment that there could be just a bit more than this (the current state of affairs as it is) to life, and the kids? In our lives, even if we had only dared to do things differently, or reason these things out, evenly? To apply ourselves to the tasks? No, not the ones in the sky, but, like, to ask why, like. Why did it all have to come to this, and so fast? No, I don't have the answers either, just the questions to ask you, Freda.

So, the Elk would have gotten himself kicked out of the church, unceremoniously so, of course, it did hurt a lot, on his backpack. Or even worse than that, the rear-end part. For what did you ask? For having the unmitigated gall to write books, storybooks of sorts. A fictional storybook included in the pack, at that, about love, sex, relationships, and such. He then tried to sell that book to those said church folks. Thought that, perhaps, he could make a little extra cash here and there in the process of leading and steering. Or a lot of it, like thieving Steven, the prophet, (beware of him). Couldn't hurt anyone, anywhere. Well, so you'd think after reading this pair... Can't do that sort of thing any... not in this church, namely... "Around these parts," he was told, we go out and get a job, and fast. "Even in the cold?" "Freeze zzz, a real job," they say, as if it's the only thing that's going to be an answer to the prayers they'd prayed. Well done, at last, you've prayed, as real folks around here do, and do, do...

Especially real church folks like them, and yes, you. Isn't that true? "Yes." That's what we do around here, that's what you're going to do too, my dear. We're real folks, real folks go out job-hunting on spokes, and searching, of course. After we're done with praying, for said jobs, just saying! Those other kinds of jobs that other kinds of folks will have to go out and find ways and means of creating and providing for us. It's not about us doing it for ourselves, nor facing the fuss over wealth (no, more like the lack thereof). They'd better do it. Like, go out and create those jobs for us, the prophets. Because we'd prayed and asked our god for it, and the comforts. It's now your job to go out, create, and deliver it to us, first and foremost. You had better do it because you don't want what's coming to you next if you don't. (Spit). We'll pray to our god again, and she will come and get you out front, often, for not doing what you ought to do; for not providing us the jobs that we needed to earn our food, as you already know you ought to. So that we may go out, (or come in). Into our father's churches, and with praise and thanksgiving. To worship our God and king with the gifts of our first fruits of the evening, every pay period, even. Just like she'd asked us to do and was glad, yes, it's true. "Or did she?" Come and see. She never said we should be the creators of anything, not even jobs, oh, the poor thing. A piece of work like me, I'm glad that she's in. She never asked that of us, let alone art and crafts, which could include our writings, in the creativity class. Wrong things, even, like writing books and such? No, not those again, no more books that could (possibly) earn us some real money, no handcuffs hanging on me, or better off? Bringing us lots of real money. "No pops." She never asked that of us; we dare not do such, or else, we may earn the wrath of our leaders in the house and wives. That's the very last thing that the Lord will have us doing to please her, no surprise. For sure, heaven will never see our faces for such wrongs that we would have committed and delivered against our church and moms, scrubbing away at the rocks in the rivers to the bottoms. Its leaders, too, rulers, and most importantly, the sacred rules of the said church.

So, "Four weeks," they'd said. You've got to sit down for four weeks and take a break from your positions in the church, mi bred, from the cup and bread, and play. Like, no more of you sitting up there and playing the music of the day. Really? Some kind of sanction, I'd say. Feel me? What were they even thinking that day? Were they even thinking at all? What were those positions? One might have asked, and one would have been right to at least ask or wonder about the paths. The Elk was a very busy person in the church, mi cous. A busybody, some might have even dared to say to me, like a curse. He has a way of getting into things he (seemingly) has no business getting into, like jobs, for example, and you. Jobs that (just like everything else with these folks), they were never approved of when you're going into the corks. But they'll surely approve of the money coming out, of course, and like, coming out of it and going to them, in the end. Just for instance, I'm saying this, my friend. Relationships too. The Elk tends to get into other people's re-lationships queue, like telling some of them what to do. Especially the young ones amongst them, and you. Telling them to get one, like, a rela-tionship plan. "Get one of those things and move on with the business of living, the business of life." Like, having children and wives, well, if the husband were to be the choice. Can't do that, not around these parts on these lot, tory pots, not around here, Mister Matts, but the robots are coming, my dear. Huh-huh.

Not long after arriving on the scene over there and getting himself settled in with a box of beer like... like somewhere in between them, sit-ting there. Elkhan the Elk would have gotten hold of a credit card, some-thing he never had before, you know, like, him coming in from the West Indian country yard, and all. "Now, I can go out and purchase some-thing, anything I want," so said the Elk to himself and them, with a chant. Yeah! A car was his item of choice, and off to the car-marketing plant, they went, singing and rejoicing, is what he meant. Would have gone car-hunting, you know, with one of the elders from amongst them, the chiefest of foes, I mean friends. Spotted a couple of fine-looking cars, yes, as fine as you are. The elder liked the blue, the Elk liked it too, but... But he liked the grey more than you. This was the Elk's very first at-tempt at owning an automobile, and him being that way behind the wheel. At the same time, the elder was a seasoned person in the automo-tive world, though not a proper welder — man, working on the girls... Elk needed all the help he could get and the girls' address to get into their yard. He needed the elder's help in making a decision, you bet. He schooled him, yes, he schooled the Elk on all the reasons why the blue was the car for him and you. Of course, he bought the grey, you know him well today, the Elk, yes, he who is a wild ass son of a big-time chicken farmer around these parts. "How so?" you'd asked, and stormed her. How did he get to be so brazen on the task to, like, disarm the mis-ter? Elk would have learned over time how to use (or not use) the ad-vice and instructions that they were giving him. Based mainly on his assessments of the real value of such, towards the win. He got the car, yes, the one he'd chosen above him, her, and the rest. It's performing great, everybody likes it too, even the Ape. So, now it's luck that's running into him from the blabbermouths of the day. Every chance this and other such person gets (or didn't get), they'd venture into telling him just how "lucky" he was. It's not the blessing effects anymore, as was the custom on the prayer floor above, before. With him and his kind of people, you know, like, the crook, and your... "So, I am lucky now," said the Elk from within the bore. But then, the harder he worked and tried to do such things, the luckier he found that he was getting to become with them. Even at getting into the inns, come to think. He, therefore, just went right along doing his things, his way. Then, one day, there was to come that other occasion, like, let's just say it this way, when the Elk himself had gotten what was to become his very first real long-term job, from you, no? "No." Anyway, let's go along, boo, boo. Again, he talked to them, and he told it to the elder and a few of the other friends. Yeah, we have a way of telling them everything, every time.

So, the Elk told them about it, looking for an "amen" and an acquit, no denying it. I know, he too is one from among them, and you, we as a people, never learned "Nuttn," my friend. Nothing at all. So, he told him about the job he'd gotten himself, and the elder wanted details. "It's nothing too grandiose, really, just a machine operator's job on the house," feel me? A sewing machine operator's kind of job to toast.

"Oh no," he said and sobbed. "I don't think that a man like you should be doing that type of work for a job," like, like, my job is not like your job. You can do much better than that, working for the mob, Bob. Well, not really, that's not how the conversation went, willy-nilly, no. Bob was out working at his job, at the time, yes, but he was talking to the Elk and me, of course. (Nice smile).

Meanwhile, the Elk was there thinking to himself in style and wondering how to better shape the machete with the file. "Have you got such a job for me?" he dropped the asked as a question on his kid's knee, or any other kind of job, for that matter, to see. Have you got any such thing, even one of those things to offer me, or anyone else? He was musing about this within himself. Again, though, you know what he ended up doing, right? Ten years later on, he was still there doing just that one, the sewing job he'd gotten got, and screwing around with fat. You know, like, operating sewing machines and screwing around a round of beer on the center pole beams. Until tragedy came in and struck him on the but... but, I mean, the Elk then found it necessary to move on. He decided to upgrade his driver's license to be able to operate one, yeah, one of those heavy vehicle things, come on! Again, the word got around and into the ears of this, as well as other people clown in the "we-group" of his, down-home. Hiss, yes, okay, now put away the frown. The Elk had not bothered to tell us who told them this; this time, it was way too embarrassing for him to twine around his fist. I'd suppose so and continued twisting the twine around these fingers of mine. Yeah, squirm and hiss, Ms. Whyne. Even now, as we're here looking back at it, over the toast, I can see why. Oh, my lord, suppose...? So, this time is going to be different than the others, right? Go on, keep your mouth closed, and shut in while sleeping and dreaming of fools tonight.

"That's not a good profession," they say. "Truck drivers have a way of dying too often on the roadway. They have to go on long-distance trips sometimes, too, some that tend to take them away from their family, and you... "True." From 'the church,' and for long periods in the queue." And yes, away from you, too, Aunt Sue, no? Well, fire up the engine, let's go, tell. "And that's not good at all for you," so they say. On and on, the rhetoric was to continue along, against this line of work for winning food, and for our moms doing good.

As you already know, but might not care to say, the Elk had to take note of those things and make a sensible decision to win and show the way, okay? He was made the church's Sunday School bus driver not many months later. That was because he was the logical choice there. The only one among them with a heavy vehicle driver's license, and all the other certifications necessary to drive such vehicles away from them and theirs, like the bison. Did that for well over a decade in accumulated years, until...

Until he rubbed them the wrong way yet again. Happened when he got the fabulous idea that he could write books and sell them to make some extra money here and there to spend, among the crooks, among them, even. So, he wrote one, then another. Now he's up to six and comes face to face with a new challenge on the ladder, sticks, or two of the brothers. (Spits). He was having grave difficulty in writing love scenes. Not so much because he didn't know about love or seeing such scenes? "Seen." Or even about writing them well enough to have been able to see things as they were from in between... You know, like, seeing such things often enough from in between the peeping scenes that he would be able to do it. No, it wasn't that, nor was he in any way unfamiliar with the subject matter of the day. Who'd asked? Oh, you again. It was more out of fear, out of the fear of what other people may come to think about him, and such things as what he thinks about those matters on the string. Particularly, those same kinds of "Other people," and their daughters too, were in the vehicle. Look, isn't she cute? "Yes." Secondly, he also wanted to try another style of writing, like writing in the first person, which, at that time, was the right thing, as he'd never done before. At the same time, too, there was a competition going on on your favorite tube. Well, no, not quite so. Trying to get new, unpublished books published on Amazon Kindle is true. "Amazon Scout" was the name, as it was given to us, to go and sell on the way out. The Elk wanted to enter his book into the competition, to try and win Dell, if nothing else (to win it from). Fifty thousand words, or more, was what they were after, but he was done telling his story in about thirty-five thousand words and fewer. He wanted to get the book enrolled in the competition, though. So, back to the drawing board he had to go, to fix them and try to win friends. He managed to get to forty-eight thousand plus words, and he took a chance at entering the book into the competition just before the door closed against the door jam. Yes, before the deadline for entry occurred, they accepted it, Ma'am. He was elated, to say the least. In the meantime, though, as the competition continued down the line, slow. Down towards the drawing of the winners after the show. He was to be found doing in-house promotion of the book and preparing the people for the release of the sweet lotion on the nook when that time should come around. He told many of them, very many. Among other things, he was heard telling them that he was going to get kicked out of the church, "Whenever this new book gets out," he said, "or worse." The more he talked about it, the more the interest mounted in the cockpit. Everybody wanted a copy of it. Everybody except a few here and there, of course. The price, perhaps? He would have been thinking this because… Well, you know the facts. But other revelations were to come to light, bursting out of the darkness one night. Some folks who'd bought copies of the previous works didn't want to buy any more that night, of course. "Because of what, wasn't it good?" He'd asked a number of the otherwise good ones or twos. Weren't the others good, or was it the price? Again, he was asking this because the new book was to cost a bit more than the others before it. Then came the big reveal. "I haven't even read the first one that I bought from you yet." Yes, that was the answer he'd gotten get. This, he was told by more people than one, Sir. Much more than one. Which got to the inner ear of the Elkhan and the bear man, to get him thinking again about the reasons. What kind of people do things like that to them, and why? Why would they do that to a rather nice guy? Go on, laugh as much as you like, this too shall pass you by, but… The first part of the question was a bit easy to answer for the man because everybody knows the answer to that one, and fast. Everybody already knows that; one can and does hide knowledge from this kind of people, even in the classroom of the feeble (bowl of porridge). This particular kind of people. One can and does hide knowledge from these people in the pages of… (of all things) books, like that one, even. No less than hanging it on the hooks and racks, with the weevil feeding. "And why is that you'd asked? It's because *"don't none of them evva read nuttn."* I mean, none of us ever read anything. Not even our favorite book of them all from within the worship hall. Yeah, man, look, there it is, that book is still hanging beside Freddie Mac's picture, on the wall. They don't read it either. They never did bother to read "Nuttn," not anything Ms. Freda, ever. So, no need for you to worry about them reading this one to be clever, or anything else. Nor about writing a little *bit a "letta" to a nedda bredda*, if you want. Go on out, or come right on in and write your letter to try and say everything that I have got on my mind to say to Erica. Or something else, anything, they won't know. Not unless somebody tells them which way to go? Oh! Wait a minute, no, you will probably need to worry a bit about that part, my friend. That person, the "somebody" person? That somebody is itching right now, this minute even, to go do her favorite thing, and worsens... Yes, the telling thing, you know them. Well, not you-you, this is not about you, you're some sort of different and special thing to do, do, you do read a lot, right? Not too big on talking and chit-chatting tonight, but reading is your kind of thing to be needing, right? So, you know very well that we're just stretching things a bit here, to make a point, out of these imported beers, right? But you also know darn well that, as for the rest of our people on the lot, Tory Bell? (foot pants). Like that, like him, and me, and you. Advance. *We don't "Nevva read nuttn",* yeah! I said it. Nothing at all, not even our favorite book of them all. Except on Sunday mornings at the altar call, perhaps. A few verses here and there, as we may be asked, so to do, and share, in the morning services too, be aware. But as for the other part of the statement? That too was to be a torment. That's what got the Elk thinking in Technicolor jogging shoes and felt that are meant... Why would anybody, even them, Bobby? Why would they bother to buy the book if they weren't going to read it this evening? Look. That question was answered, too, really quickly, not long afterward, like, after it bit me. They bought the book only to "Support him, and the lord." It's a nice thing to do, one might suppose so to say, and wink in accord, (at you).

But if you'd respected yourself and the value of a dollar bill, over there in the money till under somebody else's shelf. Your dollar, even. Respect the effort of the person who'd labored on the task of writing the book, to begin with, and whom you said you were buying the item from, to provide support (sit down on the dim with... I mean, man, sit).

You wouldn't have done that, mi scout, like this? Just pay your hard-earned money for it, then take it and throw it in the corner pit where it is likely to stay and rot in...it.

You wouldn't have done that if you were a person who puts value on anything. "Like what, like...?" "Your money, perhaps." So now, the book is out, yes, the new one, and has reached the hands of the many, nuance, and is gone. Running off and after many of those people, and corn. They're reading it and calling around the vehicle to snitch. This one, and yes, that one too, and telling the story of, guess who?

"Telling the story of Jeezas, right?"

"No, you, Iddie hat, not that, bright, not the story of Jesus, but they were telling each other what's written in the book, as she always does whenever she's phoning you, and cooks... like cooking the food. The panel discussion got heated up to a fever pitch in no time. Like, while peeling off the skin of the onions and getting ready to finish cooking my favorite dish after washing the fish with vinegar and lime, well, hers and mine. It's getting judgmental now, and then, the first call was to come home to the author, from them. "Great book," said the caller to him, now look, and wink. "Good evening," he said, while she was leaving the Bred... feeling, "very good." It was a very good report for the author to believe in; he couldn't have been happier, even after. "Brother," said the caller, "you hit it out of the park this time. I can't stop reading these lines." Then came the chime, "I'm at the seventeenth chapter." This was said in response to a query from the author's hand in proper, as to how far along in the book the person had reached since she began to read. Good again, very good, just like preach, as I'd understood... him to be. The only problem with that was that it wasn't the end of the report, not yet. We were only just getting started, to sweat, of course. Hours later, other calls were to come ringing through the Gator's gate, sir, and coming home. From folks like ours, some of whom didn't even bother to... "You know, like to — "What, to buy a copy from him and you?"

"Yeah, you're right! Who told you?" They wanted to voice their opinions, though, but not before making sure and verifying whether the author was a Christian Bro.

"I'm a man in search of God," was the reply to them off-chord. "Still searching," he said, before the continuation of the queries ahead. Are you that type of person, too, mi bred? Come along with me, let's go a-searching then, for some more money to buy milk and bread. For some answers, too, to try and see how to get a monster through to them. More surprises were to come, too, like those coming in from, guess who? Yes, true. Like, when the very first one who'd called him and her, with nothing but high praise for the book for sure. She who was (at the time) well on the way through to the eighteenth chapter, and crying. No, not for that, but with the joy of the high end. Now, she's heading towards the end, yeah, nearing the outback door to the pasture, and the "Amen." Now, though, that same person is calling back again to say what she wants the author to know about him that they didn't like, like, something that was said in the third chapter one night, near the beginning.

Or perhaps it was in the way it was said, to improperly clabb...clasp her on the ear near the head in the nodding. Could it be so, mi bred? Or could it be that this person was just there to add her voice to the growing chorus? One might have thought so and poured out a cuss... cursing out their guts. A chorus that was, by then, becoming a mass choir of sorts. Or more like a mob squad of smart? Something, (or not). Voicing their disapproval of that single aspect of the book they were in, to the class, and this particular person just wanted to add her voice also, to the streams of discontent, now hastening on to flow over the waterfall cement, like, just in case? Could it be, could it possibly be so? Why then did you not have an issue at first, Ms. Flo, like, when you'd read it in the third chapter, and the verse? Now that you are nearing the end of the twenty-eight-chapter book, though, in the pasture too, and on every green grass that grows, over you, your head, and to your curse. After finding out that other folks, some other folks from the in-group, have issues with the book. Or more like that very small passage of the book.

Suddenly, you now feel the need to add your voice to the chorus in the nook, to say, yes, me too. I, too, have issues with it that way. Yes, I do. Because of what, and who? Because you don't want to be seen as the odd person out of the kit bean, like — "Like the kitty cat?"

"Probably true, mi pops. Well, this son of a big-time chicken farmer here," said Elkhan the Elk to the wild beer. "I am an Elk from the south side of the Polish to a shine pole. I don't have a problem being the odd person out of the fold in this and some other types of situations, cold, Inez." So, get out of the way, folks, here comes the Elk down the holy smokes, and the good old Saint; Saint Nick himself, doesn't want anything to do with any part of him this time, on the shelf. But...

Chapter four

Who Would You Rather Be? Piper or the payer?

The man who pays the Piper, they say, calls the tune today.

If that is true, and as the records tend to show to me and you, it is. Strive, therefore, to become the piper-payer. Not just the fiddling piper, always, like you seemed so likely to be, and glorying in it, all day, oh. So, whenever you're there, praying to your Gods for help and providence. How is it that you always want to be the piper and nothing else? Never the payer of pipers, no, and hence, *don't none a yuh gon* become a survivor, in the end. No, you're not going to survive to make it to the end like that. Don't you think that your god could? If she could do the one, she should have been able to do the other also, no?

So, perhaps your present predicament (our present predicament) is not so much a reflection on our Gods and our saints in Hilfiger lengths... but more so on us, and you again, gentlemen. On the dads and dames too, no? Not true? Now, let me try and put it all in layman's terms here for you, peradventure you will be better able to see your way through. If you hear your God (or gods) say: Bring all the tithes and offerings into the storehouse and prove me now (which means, to test me, or try me). See if I will not open the windows (and the doors too, probably). See if I will not open the windows of heaven and pour out a blessing for you, that you will not have enough room to receive it. Wasn't that what the scripture says to you? When was the last time you read it? Then, after hearing those sayings, straight away, right after hearing him say it, and even after saying those things yourself that day, on the seats. You go on to pray the same prayer that you've been praying like, like, forever, and since. Like, even before yesterday morning drinks. More like: forever to stay on needles and pins, for all of your life, I'd say, you have been praying that same prayer. Go on, call me a liar, or go back to your prayers; praying for jobs, on the choir, and jobs only, and getting nothing else but jabs on the jobs, not even riding the pony. Not even so much as good pay coming to you from the said job of the day, my homey. The robots are coming, though, coming your way for sure. But yes. In the meantime, you've been seen there, praying that very same prayer in my ear, and still finding that you're always at the same place, my dear. In your life, in your house. In your community, in your country, in the world. That place, as it turned out, where you're at, and I, too, yes, we're all at the bottom of the see-through, at the bottom of everything, isn't that true? Yes, and it's not a good place to be, to begin with. Well, at least, not for me or him, we're the dimmed "Wheats" within. But there seem to be other constants here to try to see through. You're always able to get a job, it would have seemed, on the square habit, and those beams. "True." No matter how much you hated it, the fact is, you've got it. Could it be that one gets what one prays for, even you, and from her, too? Could it be that your god answers prayers, in truth? Yours even? Remember, you didn't even bother to specify the type of job you wanted while you were there, praying and asking as you did. You just asked for a job to rawtid, wearing the bib, probably. Well, there, you've got your job alright, my dear. Not bad, your god has been faithful to you, so it's your turn now to go, go out, and show the rest of them how it's done, nope? How faithful are you to your god? Do you believe that she can do more than just get you a job? Do you believe that she's able to make you an employer of people, like that, Bob, over there by you? Like, like, like giving jobs to people who needed jobs, whether or not they'd prayed to God for one? This god or any other?

Do you think that would be something worth proving your god on, and not on the bother of the other man, mother? Why not try that then, even for one fleeting moment? By doing this, perhaps you would be seen as honoring your god, showing her off in a light that will make others want a piece of her, and you would be glad. Therefore, people would want to get to know her even half as much as you do (these offers). You could also be learning something new and valuable about your God in the process, too, couldn't you? A disaster. Something that could contribute greatly to taking and making you the head. The real head this time, and not just the bed head that you have imagined sleeping in, in your mind. The head that you like so much to boast that you are, contrary to what everyone else everywhere knows to be the truth, and by far. That you, as well as I, yes, we're all singularly, or collectively, whichever way we may want to look at it, to see the tea, Leigh, we're the tail. The whippy, hair-wagging end of the tail. But that too can be changed without fail, this I do believe.

Your God, my God, alongside me, my many efforts, and yours, you'll agree, are well able, of course, that's why I bother. But, oh my brother! If it is true that "He who pays the piper calls the tune." Why wouldn't you want to be the payer, rather than the piper playing the fool there with the man on the moon, and like, always? Strive to be the payer of pipers, I'd say. Yes, we can. Don't forget when you are praying for those jobs, though. Robots are coming, coming along the road to Benbow, slow.

Chapter five

The Man Has Shown You.

You complained about having to endure great hardships at the hands of the other man, who forced you to build his now-flourishing society on the stolen lands. Out of the place where, once there was only wilderness and trees, now you want payback for it, like this, and these. "Oh, please!" Yes, you talk about reparations and repatriation, which sounds good indeed, to the faraway nations on their knees. You curse that man out of his van and give him a piece of your mind, every chance that you get (or didn't get). It's probably the very reason why you seem to have so little of it left; the "mind" thing that is, you bet. A mind of your own is a forbidden concept. You tell the man what you think of him, all the time, just not in his hearing, but still, on the hidden line. You cursed the man out of his clothes and told him just what you thought of him. Color him red, and black not, but yellow, purple, and pink, somewhere between his head top and the kitchen sink, now, here for you, is a drink, wink. "He's a beer barrel," you'd said. "He drinks a lot and beats his wife. Quarrels all the time, throughout the night." He's not like you; there's nothing to compare him to. That man is now driving the old Ford Fiesta that you threw away, his transportation whenever he goes to collect his pay down by the apartment complex overlooking the bay. His property, all of them. Money in the bank for him and his children, to the nth generation of them. But as for you, what do you do? While you, your mamma, and all your ill-begotten children in proper, live on the upper floor of those said beachfront apartments, of the goner. You're pushing a crisp, shiny Mercedes-Benz on the way out there to go pay him the rent, "Because..." Yes, because of things like this, you're hip and classy. Quite unlike that colorful drunk-a-lot in the Fiesta of his. The one he'd picked up out of the trash heap near the properties, now, look at him, he's a whip and trashy. "He ain't going nowhere." But as for you? You're already there, way up top in the air. So, young man, what are you going to do with your plans from here? Who are you going to immolate from now on, which of the two, or way too many other ones? How long will you stand? How long will you be able to stand like a man, like you want to do so very badly? How long? Ask that man, the old man, or his daddy. Your old man, even, it's him, your old man has got the answer there in his hand to spin around me, no? Yes, well, so to you it would seem, but does he even understand?

So, you delight yourself in giving the man a piece of your mind? I'm about to give you a piece of my mind, too. Even before I'm done, you might be ready and willing to do to me, just like you've said you're going to do to that one. Yes, to him, but only more. But I'm going to tell you anyway because someone needs to tell you the score; peradventure you will hear it and make the necessary adjustments to the door, way... No, not the door, but what I meant to say is, to your way of thinking. To your ways of doing things, or not doing anything, to your ways. Change your ways, I'd say, and begin to live, like him, even. Well, in some of those ways of his, at least, so that you may begin to live this time in peace. That man you see right there, you may do well to leave him alone and spare. Yeah, man! Spear him or leave him be. He's probably the best friend you've ever had, or will ever have, from me. That man, you see, has been showing you (yeah! I will too), he has been showing you and will show you still, what you ought to do, and the will. And like, how to do it too, to fulfill...

Like, to fulfill your purpose, or to live and survive at the very least, even in the circus. But you're fully dunce, so you will not be taught, not even an ounce, no, you won't learn a fa... no, leave it at that. He has been telling you, though, telling you all along what you need to know, like what you need to do, and get done to get you securely home, and through the loops. But you will not listen to anyone, oops! So, now you want him to give you some of his many wonderful things, like some of the states that he has built with blood, sweat, and tears coming from him. Not just your blood, your sweat, and your tears to spin, but his blood also, his sweat and his tears, yes, his too had to flow. Don't forget that he had to come in and tame the wildlands for you. The lands on which he has built those fabulous cities up and out of the plantation's shoot, cities that you now crave and covet like a brute. Many of his kind of people suffered and died in the process. It wasn't just you and your kind who had suffered and died out west. If you're sitting there thinking you're going to talk him into handing over one, two, seven, or even eight of his cities, any city that he has built at a high cost to himself and his kind of kiddies. Then you're a bigger fool than you seem to be, in the minies, and everybody knows that you are. Except you, of course, and you would probably deserve it. Not just what you've gotten, but what is coming to you, still... Sit. You're so busy fooling yourself that you cannot even notice that part of the will. Everywhere they went, they had to pay their portion of the rent, in blood, even.

The death rate, they said, was very high among the first arrivals. Those same ones, even, the other men's survival, it wasn't all dependent on you. Low life expectancy and high infant mortality. Diseases, the most dangerous diseases, as well as wars of various sorts and fees, yes, those fees of his. These and other things contributed to a great loss of life among them, too. Furthermore, here's the real score: that wasn't why the man built his beautiful cities on the shores of rivers and seas. To then turn around and give it up to people like this, and these? Hand it off to them, and you and those. No, it ain't going to happen, like so. Oh, man! "Go and wipe your nose." He's not going to give back the "land he'd stolen from those 'other people' and their fighting men." Like you love to say, constantly, amen. It was to build his cities that he took it. I'm sure he'll not give it over to you as is, not without a fight from his fist, and you can go on deluding yourself tonight, like, into thinking you can take him on in a fight, and win. Go right on, that's a good thing. Your God, you say, is on your side. Well, hooray! Let's go for a ride. But what if you should wake up one of these days to find out and see the light that your God, in whom you've placed such great confidence last night, and bragged like a braggart, in tights? That God was given to you in his defense and regard, and by, guess who? Yeah, you got it right, my friend. I know you're mad right now, and so are the gods, your God, even, wow. If she wasn't coming to get me and everybody else before, and Steven, she sure is on the way now, even at the door, and peeping in. So, go right on, take him to task with your right hand. Take your fight to that man in the name of your God and your mom. Or your myriads of gods, or go jump into some boiling wax because... Frankly, the two might turn out to be the very same, and one again.

God could be at work on this, too, don't you think? I've heard some great sermons preached in my time. Great prayers too, and rhymes. But what if your god, the very same one you are praying to and asking those great things of, for your comfort? Suppose she decides to answer your prayers and help you out. What if she should come to your rescue with a shout? What if it is she who is at work now, even in this thing that you are getting so riled up about, wow! Or the entire load in this pile of "Scrap-bookery" that you're now reading aloud and out? What if it's all your God's doing?

But you're so set in your way, so afraid of change that you dare not touch anything different today, Sue Hingh? So, I am very sure you are thinking the same thing again, "God doesn't work like that." Could you not be there, making yourself busy, canceling every new thing she's doing in your life, canceling out the very things you've asked her to do for you last night, like your husband or your wife? While she's in the process of doing it. Couldn't you be there busily cancelling out that very thing with you in it, and whistling? Well, couldn't you?

...

Go right ahead L'il Sissy, go buy those building blocks for me. Then purchase the plaques too (both of them), even. One for the local building at the congregation house, the one that is now in construction mode. The other one is for the headquarters church down the road. The new church buildings are going up as I'd supposed, everybody is excited about them, of course, the new church buildings, and the new cup. Yes, everybody is pitching in; they're all playing their part to get the kitchen in and the roof up. You must do likewise. You must play your part too (whether or not you can afford to), you'd better, or else, they'll shame you. That's one of their most valued tools used to blame whom? Yes, you. They're not shy about using it either. The other church building is going up, too, the "headquarters church." Shuts! Man, what a sight to behold, that church! Ooh! It is a good one for a man who's so brave and bold. "You're going to have to do your part here, too, Sis," you were told last night after the choir practice. As you already know, you must, just like everyone else, and the household. Who's going to stop you anyway? It's your money, your hard-earned money from your pay, it's yours to go out and play. You can do with it whatever you like, and you sure would like to have your name on one of those stones, written bold and bright! Anchored there on the side wall of the church building when it's all done tonight. A plaque on the inside wall as well. Guy-url, that thing is looking fantastic. It's going to be there forever, just like plastic, even into eternity. Bishop deserves it; that man deserves the very best. Look at it, look at all the things he has done for us. Look at all those churches he's planted and built upon all the fuss over praying for the house.

Bishop really did build a lot of churches, and a lot of families, too, out of our purses, not his. Church families, of course, as with the other types of families, though, no. "No?" "Yes." "I know." But that's quite another story for other times and places to go. I would have seen what became of them, some of them, really, I'll tell you some more about them later, probably. What they thought of the good bishop and all in the end. Do they still consider him a family member and a friend? And what about their real families, what was to become of their own flesh and blood families in the meantime, amen? Hmm, hmm, hmm. Yeah, man! I'm humming off a little song and pad-patting my heels and toes here, folks.

What have we done, though, I mean, really, what have we done thus far, for little Willie? How much have we achieved as a people over there, the place where we are more than half sure that we're going on these very old church vehicles and the chairs? What have we built, other than churches? Tiny churches, perhaps, on other people's pieces of ground, as it is. Or, on what's left of our fast-wasting-away little pieces of ground near the cribs. How much have we invested in our people, our children, even? What if we had invested a fraction of that which we've invested in building churches into our children's cranial purses? What effect would that have had on them, and us as a people, on our hopes for the future, and the riddance of the weevil? Yet, while the churches go up, preachers get fatter and richer via the collection cups. Well, perhaps not, not all of them, because you're not, neither rich nor fat, for the most part. The few resources we have, though, flow away and continue to flow from us to them, the real them. No? Yes, all the time, and through the preacher's hands, no? "No, not from yours and mine." "Okay, see you next time." The preacher buys himself some credentials with your money, then he goes out and buys (or builds) *fii dem gals*, churches. Lots of churches for those girls of his, again, with your money from the purses, and was to have gotten himself pushed up some "never before existed" ladder, to become a name, or something another. A revered person in your mind. Your brother and the Dame, in your community, gave him the eye. In your country. "Your wasting away, country." The very one that gave you your birth and sustenance, until you were able to get out of there and get rid of me. Like, to be gone from there and thence. As soon as you could leave, you did just that: you left the cribs. Tossing a stone behind you, and vexing with his... tone (it down, mi peeps). "I will not go back to that god-forsaken place," you'd said, and have not gone back since, for the bed. Nor have you sent anything back except. Yes. Except for that little morsel for your mamma, and a parcel, now and then, perhaps, over the paths to, if ever. But you ain't never going back there, ever. Because no good can come of that place, you'd said, and clever. Scratch your head, sword... about, and swear on your bredda, yes, my brother. "But as for this! This place right here, where I am, right now, this is it; this is the place to sit." As for that brash Bish? He's no novice. Bishop has done very well for himself, hasn't he? He has built a lot of things in his time, and a cemetery. No, not for me and mine, I'm not in that much hurry... to go trying. But what if he could catch a new vision now and start building some other types of things somehow? Like schools, for example, no, no more songs to sing, and go dancing over the children, and trample them. Colleges, too, like scientific research facilities for them and you. Something for the children too, like universities, and I mean the real types of universities here, like those of the Ivy League types, for example, my dear. Not so many of the fake types that he and his kind have been seen putting together, though, just to edify and certify themselves in poppy shows, or the eyes of their unsuspecting congregations and believers below. Why not start to focus on the real job of building a country on the rivers? So that we can leave hers and go over there to deliver ours, like, a continent for a people, our people. A place they can truly call their very own under the sun, and come home in the vehicle, where they can begin to become masters of their destiny. Why not? Is this too much to ask of Lot for me? Speaking of places under the sun, see this place right here? Did you know, did it ever occur to you that this place that you have come to love so very much, and would not give up on all the bicycles in Beijing, in the rush? Did it occur to you that this place doesn't love you nearly as much as the songs that they sing? Never did, never will. Did it occur to you that this fabulous place right here was once a rugged old wilderness for bears? But some folks came in on a ship, saw it, loved it, then set out to take and claim it, and claim they did, at a high cost to themselves and the pig. As well as to others, including us and our kids, among many others. So, now you see here a city grand and glorious, you like it loads and want it even more loads than those. "All of it." You ain't never gonna get it, never gonna get it, ever. But you can get the shell out and go build your own, just like they have been telling you to do and have done. For too long a time, too, even. But your ears are tough; you are hard of hearing. So, you sit there comfortably in your miserable chair and bearing, with it, like you don't even know it, (not caring). "Oh, sheet." Or you might have chosen to forget about it, like, that you're miserable. I beseech you, therefore, brothering. Take some time, study, and learn the rhymes. Go learn something, anything other than thine. That man, the other guy whom you loved so much to hate, unlike you and me. He has thought of some things in his time, like parsley on a plate, honey too, from the bee, and lime. He has seen some things, like the many things you love to eat, all the time. He sure has a long memory. As for you and me? Yeah! I know; we've got some long things too. Look, can you see who? Like, "Long time nuh see you... 'Buddy,'" and a few, if any other long things have those of us, and you, sadly. People like me, and you, and him. So, boast as much as you like about that long thing, the one thing that you might be found to be having that may be "long," alright. But it may amount to nuttn tonight, sorry, ma-hite, I meant to say, it may not amount to anything, really, in the long run (or short). In the grand and glorious scheme of other things to add to the sum or quart. "But what?" Apart from all those things, like those things that the other man has already done. He has been teaching you some things and more "some," even in the long run, like, while running you out with the words from his mouth, against the tongue. But you will not learn. You're in a far better place today to go out and build your demanding city. In your own country and whatever else it may be that you see fit to build pretty, and go punchy with it, if you want to. You're in a far better position than he was when he first ventured out to go and build his lovely cities and countries. His effort was done with many trials and errors, as well as learning while on the go, for that fellow. Going to get paid back in multiplied sum, thing, from what you owed him, no? "Yes." You, on the other hand, all you now need to do is go out and learn the now tried, tested, and proven crafts from the other man, throughout... Those that man (as well as others, all other men, at last) has already done. They would have gone through the process of building and creating it fast and made 'em run. He has, they all have. They have perfected and documented it for whosoever will come and study it and learn, of course. Including you and Kern, off chords. He has written it down in books and built schools and universities where people can just go and look, and learn how to cook it up like these. Go get the know-how, including you, but oh how...! As for you, you ain't too big on the book thing, the schooling, or the learning fling. So, you choose instead to give up your little piece of ground, to go on over and sojourn in that other man's cities and towns. Meanwhile, the fire burns, and you sing beautiful songs, dance, and protest church romance. That's the thing to do to get you to where you want to go, best. "Like, to France?" Yeah! Francine is what I mean. If you're there waiting to go glorying in that block of the history month thing, which you like so much to talk and boast about as the icing on the cake, at that particular time of the year, for goodness' sake, Hingh, no doubt, a mistake. Every year, points you to these as evidence of your achievements over here, where you live. Your contribution towards the common good of all mankind, and those sitting there, is still behind the baby crib. If that's the evidence of your great achievements, then it's the surest sign ever that you haven't done nearly enough for *yuh bredda*. Yes, oh yes, my dear beloved brother. Now that your errors are catching up with you, the errors of your doings too. You want to stay, and the other man is saying. "No way, go, go away." But you? You say no, "I'mma gonna stay, comes what may." Then, "comes what may," was to come, caught you with your pants down, whatever else there was that could be pulled down, was down. Everything is now down, and they started doping you and throwing you around, into the dungeons, too, for little or no reason. "Phew." Or so to you it would have seemed because you can't ever seem to see anything at all anyway, other than in dreams, and in the play, perhaps. So, you continued on, business as usual. You and your man with the gal-dem, and that other new gal, the other girl's girlfriend. Still demanding things that you will never get from them, could never get. Although everyone else knew that much, you still don't know it's flush, yet. But you will soon, just wait there and see (the man on the moon). So now the man is taking to hitting you where it hurts the most, like, hitting your children (the very best of them) up against the post. They take and spoil them, then shoot and kill them, in the streets, even, and yet. You will not listen; you will not learn. It's not because the man doesn't love you like you've been saying, Kern. That man may be there loving you loads, even in these sayings, and the codes. He has been telling you and showing you, and being very patient with you, too. "Go back to where you came from," he said. But you? You replied from the open in your head, "At least I've got somewhere to go back to, you don't." So right, so very right you are, both of you, two counts. The man is saying to you: Go back to your place and go build it up into whatever you want it to be, even with help from me. The help is already there in the form of acquired skills, whether he tells you to fill. Teaching tools and best practices are there, too, and the rules and technical knowledge. Know-how, too, is all at your fingertips. "Cool, let's go to college to learn more about these." But you're not into building things, you're into consuming things, so go right on consuming those things, until you are outright consumed, even on his Whisky drinks. And yes, the other part of that statement may also be correct in some extended texts. "You don't have anywhere to go back to," you'd said to the man from Back-to. "At least I have." Let's say that that is true, why then are you? Why are you asking the man to give up the only place that he's got and can call his very own, too? No matter what you might think about the way he came by his lone shoe? It's his. How are you now going to see it as fair game for him to give it up to you and go back? Go back to where? It's, in fact, you who needs to get up off of that thing and go back, my dear. Go back to your place, go build it up, and make it into whatever you want it to be, in haste. Yeah! In your face, from me. Just like this place, even. Yes, you can, yes, we can, yes, any and every one of us can, can...

Here we have it, these people who are so afraid of progress, afraid of everything but the old dress, no? "No, not to undress, at..." "I know." So much so that they do "nothing," other than nothing, and beg, perhaps, and steal, and borrow. Ha-ha-ha-have mercy on us, Holy Father. Oh! You thought I was laughing? No, I'm not. If it weren't so serious and blasting, it would have been laughable. But...

Chapter six

Black Mother Prays

While black mothers pray, black fathers go away. Black sons were the ones who were made to pay, and black daughters became single, praying types of black mothers, probably. But then again, pardon me, probably not.

Here's a group of folks who would have left their various places. Most (if not all of them) leave because the situations and circumstances in their original place of business were, at best, not to their liking or taste, my Sis. They migrate, "for a better life," they say; I'm going to look for better for myself and my family today. This is a common theme in these communities, yay. Then all of us got to New Jerusalem on the bus, as I'd guessed; to the new worlds, and the comfortable address. It's the land of promise and opportunity where those things come first, and it's very pretty. Quickly, very quickly, we forget. We swapped out the family we once knew, the ones we once had, and would have left back home for you. The very ones whom we'd said were the reasons why we were migrating; to go look for bread and better, for ourselves and our family, yes mi bredda, and Gracelyn. But we swap them out, replacing them with a new family, a church family, plan, of course. Some kinds of scouts who are now packed, crammed, and (quite conveniently) very close at hand. Those who are just like us and would have been here in the new lands for the same reasons as we are. "To find a job and to make some money for themselves, and Bob Weabar." Their families, too, and streetcars. So, now we're here, we've found the job that we came here for, my dear. But before we'd gotten to that part, the part about getting the job, unscrewing the corks. We would have gotten to meet some rather familiar kinds of folks. Folks who are just like us in many ways (no jokes) for the same reason and purposes as we are. They were the very ones who would have invited us out to a good and acceptable place. Like, to a church for instant coffee taste; that's as acceptable as they come to disgrace, right? Okay, no case, ma-hite. But we were welcomed there with open arms and a seat at the table that night. Got invited to join the "family," and the fight. We did and got, not "a job to close out the gig," but got us prayed for. Great anyway, my star. Now, though, unbeknownst to us or to anyone else, singing the chorus. Except for the smart Alexis among us wearing felts, of course (or not, he might prefer to wear a baseball cap). But we're now indebted to the church, to the tune of the rest of our lives, of course. Or to a heavy dose of guilt-tripping, should in case we ever get wised up and skip-a-do on out of there before it's too late to be surprised in the kitchen, with them. There'll be much more guilt-tripping to come later on, too, if we linger. Or if we should happen to go back there for any reason after leaving, and try to bring her. In the meantime, though, what this single action would have done (in effect) is double a sister's "family" at the very least, or the brother's, still there on his knees. But she hasn't even gotten her first paycheck yet, and then they got around to baptizing her and him. Then took to getting her to make vows and pledges to them. The types she was not aware of from the ages, before then, or was not fully aware of the consequences should she fail at honoring them, and quickly. She was not made aware of those consequences beforehand, my friend and boss who bit me (on the wrong hand). Some dictate that she must pay "god" (or the lord). She must pay the lord her portion of her paycheck first, before anything or anyone else, from her purse. Then come the other auxiliary groups, those who must also get their share too, oops! "Here comes the curse." But her paycheck hasn't risen from the gravy train in the basement yet. She had not sent a penny back home to those family members yet, either. Those very same family members to whom she had made those other vows while still there on the meager. Pledges, too, and promises, and that was even before she got to know anything about this new family of his. Nor had she gotten to meet them. She hasn't yet taken care of any of the new responsibilities; life in the new space here is demanding of her on the weekend.

As for the new church family? They seem to be making it a point of their duty to stay as far away from the subject of families to handle me as possible. Real families, especially you, those families who're left back home and are on their knees calling me, on the phone. "Ooh!" They're staying as far away from that subject as they possibly can, oh please, can, can... As time slips away, she becomes more and more ashamed of herself for the way things have been turning out each day, between her and the family she'd left back home to stay, no doubt. So, she stopped calling home, and then she stopped taking their calls, too. Those calls that were coming from back home, to guess who? And then, all communication was cut between her and her family. Her far-away family, yes, the real family. Far away, though, they might have been from her, you, and me. But not to worry, she's got a new family right here, here come those packages bringing in the curry, and those beloved bottled beers. Yep, you know them. But then again, she'll soon begin to discover some new things about her newfound family and friends. *They don't never do "Nuttn," mi fren, ever.* Sorry, I meant to say, "Anything," just to be clever. They never do anything, other than nothing, and wait on the lord and pray, and sing. Yay! You'll see soon.

"Do something with your life, for crying out loud." One was heard shouting at them from the top of the crowd. Anything. "Take risks," he said, well-calculated risks preferably, but risks anyhow, mi bred. Go ahead, take them now. Of course, some of you are going to get hurt, or even die, from doing risky things. "Oh my." Don't let that hinder or deter you from taking those whiskey drinks, in disguise. It'll still be worth your while as a people in the long run (away from sinning, with the wives, probably). The ones who didn't die in the pursuit of excellence, or the wrong rum, pardon me. Which is what you're after while taking those risks, well, well done. At least, so I think. Come on, man, come, take a drink. Those "someone," the risk-takers, and the rum-stink? "Yeah!" Perhaps they'll turn out to be far better, more valuable people to themselves and society at large. People that the world will want to have hanging around, not to be thought of as excess weight or baggage in the garage, a waste of space, and disposables, as U R... So, don't be so afraid of anything and everything that you continue to do nothing other than nothing. You won't take risks, you say, because you're afraid of dying. Well, okay. Surprise-surprise, I ain't lying (down), you're going to die anyway, whether or not you take those risks of the day (come.) But if you die doing something that you love, and find that you're good, and getting better at it, even if you didn't get far enough to make an impact in your chosen field before you die, while doing it, or while trying to do... do ,,,it. The effort alone in your actions, your willingness to try something different, even to a fraction of a shoelace. That alone might be enough to inspire ten young people from the next generation, people like you and me, in admiration, to risk it. Yeah! To risk something too, and hence, become something, boo, become someone, not as misfits. Then, heaven only knows what cumulative effect it might end up having on the community at large, in the long run.

...

So what? Just because you'd spent all that money on your first of ten sons, the money you hardly ever had, then comes this gnome's comb who ended up dying at graduation. Oh no! What a sad situation. Now you've purposed in your heart to never spend a single dime more on any of the other nine sons of yours. "I'm not going to go through this again," you've said. Well, amen, right, you are, mi bred. Yes, my brother, I agree, you most certainly won't go through that same experience again. Whatever you do from here on and in, too. I will even stake a bet on that and win through. Because whatever you do, you can never ensure that none of your sons will ever go to and graduate from college against you. Or even if they're going to die, they will all die. They may even die before you do. "Oh my! Is that true?" you'd asked. "Yes." A whole lot more than that could happen to, to... The fact is, Boo, you can't impact much of anything in this regard. But you can ensure you don't go through this exact sort of thing again, just by playing cards. Well, probably, and going lame. But, for sure, you can do that by not spending the money on sending another of your nine remaining sons to college, by way of the outer end of your door, to get knowledge. In so doing, you would have ensured that none of them ever died just after graduating from the college that you'd spent money sending them to, to hide and sing. Now, sigh, bat your eyes fast, and wink. But there are a thousand other ways every one of the remaining sons can do just that; go to college, if they want (to get fat). They may even prosper at it, too, who knew? But really now, what is the likelihood of that? That all the sons, if given the exact opportunity to do the same thing as the first one. Or even many things, like continuing to go to college, for example, and taking their lessons as a sample student, to achieve the proper outcome. How likely is it that every one of them will become a victim of the same misfortune as the first son? That's the difference between fortune and misfortune, as it would be in this case of parchment. That, versus returns on investments. Results that are garnered from real efforts and such things. Studies, training, practice, and such like as these, and that is. All that versus happenstance, fortune, or misfortune; that cruel vice is worth some... All of those other things that you may do in life. If you do the same thing all the time, you can expect to come away with a particular outcome or set of outcomes every time. When it comes to luck, fortune, misfortune, or happenstance, though. One can never predict the exact outcomes of those, but Rowe. Every once in a while, one (or more) of those unpleasant events will happen. That, however, such a risk of misfortune on the lot or river should not become the determining factor in your life's decisions. Nor should the plot be screwed by your fears towards her, in derision.

Suppose another man has one son; should he spare and shelter him? His one and only son, to ensure that no evil befalls him? That would be understandable if he does, or if he tries to do so, mi cous. Wouldn't it be? But if there's a god somewhere, and sitting across from me, in the chair. If she wants you to know the answer to that and other such questions, to see the food in the pot and go share, the comments. She would (probably) have written it down somewhere in some books or the other on the stairs. But no, there's no such thing to show that fact, my brother, dear. We're all on our own, left to our own devices, and cunning the clown. Aren't we? You might want to take a look at Genesis 22 for a clue and try to see. Can you see them running after me? Oh, how she must be mad at me, though, for saying these wicked things and so... She's mad at other entities too; she sure is mad at a lot of folks these days, for just as many reasons as you and in the same ways. Or for no reason at all. "Phew!" Look at me, hand over the gaze. What do you think she thinks about entities such as NASA and other devils? These people have already gone much further than he has ever been, you know? That Nimrod fellow, for instance. That Nimrod, none rod, *"nuttn" noh goh soh rod, you mussi mad*. If you had ever flown in an aircraft, though, you would have gone much further up than Nimmo, that very long time something rod fellow had ever gone. Or could have ever gone on a slimy brick tower, and wasted products from corn — "Flour?"

"Well, maybe." But your God, who does not change, ever. Your god was so threatened by him and his kind of babies, the strangers. To the point of making some rather drastic reactionary moves and maneuvers by Nimmo? Oh gimmie oh... Did somebody play a nonsense number boy? Sorry, I meant to say a number. Somebody did play a church number on these people, boy, that's for sure. Whoa, people, be afraid, be very afraid. She's mad, she's coming to get you, too, and I'm glad. Just like she did to them, or did she? "Come and see."

Chapter seven

L ittle is Much, Well, so they say

I have some more "what if" questions for you here. I know you hate them, so you don't have to answer; I won't ask you to.

In your eyes, as you saw it, it was because the brother was stingy and hard-hit. That's why he wasn't giving you his little bit, like, the ten percent and more to trickle, like, trickling in on you, in offerings, for example. Giving it to you and the offspring to go and trample, and to theirs after them too. So that your little would be much, while his little remains little, and crushed, getting littler, and littler still. Until the "blessings" come to him to the full... fill. But as for you and yours? You want it all, of course, like the much, perhaps, and the market stalls. Or even the little, little, and yet more little. This would surely add up to be a lot of "much" for you and your kind assistance, too, to reach out and touch, you want it right now. What would you have done, though, if you were in his case of shoes? "Oh!" Yes, like, being in the same sort of situation as he was at the time, bro? Hush! Like, sipping on booze and cheap corner shop wine? But then again, maybe next time. But we all do know the facts as they apply to these and other such things. You're blessed, and he's not. So, you will never see those kinds of situations spots. Those kinds of things will not happen to you, not so fast. You won't see them through, but as for him? He will, always, and to the full, fill... because he doesn't give as much as you do, so he's not as blessed as you are and never will be.

"Little is much," so you say, and one is like, well, "O, kay!" Whose little will be much, and for whom? Whose will become the "much?" Does anyone care to answer? Do you care, though? Did you care then? I mean, really, my friend. How much so? Come now, and let us reason this out together. So, what if the brother couldn't pay? What if he really couldn't pay it, the tithes you say he must? What if it wasn't feasible because of other things that were going on in his life at the time, and such, and which he couldn't say to you or anyone else there to find, without giving every last ounce of his pride away on prime time?

"Oh, you're too proud, and that's the problem," I heard you say to all of them, but is there no virtue in self-pride of the day, self-preservation too, one might say? Or in one keeping just that little bit of one's sanity intact? What if, like, while you were there, name-calling the brother, stingy, "He's so mean," you'd said? What if the brother (or sister, for that matter) was, at the very moment, caught up smack dab in the middle of a crisis, and that other matter with the government, having real difficulty paying her way and foregoing the rice mix and the rent? "Because of..." "Whatever the reason might have been," should he still pay? Should she then pay tithes, just like you say, first and foremost? No matter what? Well, of course, "no matter what" does matter sometimes, and at this particular time in this brother's life and prime? It just might have been the only thing that mattered for the brother. Should he still pay the father? What if the brother was falling behind on his mortgage payments, for instance, just for instance, my main friends? Even on several of his many mortgage arrangements with the banks and their presidents? What if the pre-authorized payment checks he had signed and issued on the accounts at the bank were being bounced? "Insufficient funds," they might have said, even to an ounce? What if every one of those bounced checks should result in an extra sixty, sixty-five, or seventy dollars or so? What if those, too, were being tacked on to the already ballooning deficits to grow? For the benefit of the banks, you know, well, of course... Plus, the other thirty-five, forty, or more dollars to the other institutions or businesses to which those other checks were made payable (for me), as his crime was. What if those extra costs, too, were being tacked onto the deficit and on the navel for you? What if the brother (by this point) had begun to take this situation seriously to heart, and in his hands? What if he was beginning to take measures by then, to get back some semblance of control over the situation, of sorts, my friend? Or over his financial affairs to hit the restart button? What if those measures were to see him cutting the fat wherever he could? What if cutting off those meager fats wasn't enough to get things sorted out and get fatter and good, therefore, was to see him cutting back on other unnecessary things in his life? As well as some necessary ones, in some cases, of shoes for the wife? Some of which he has no business cutting back on, and on your face cloth in the wash pan? That's right. Things like insurance, for example. Home insurance, even, one can get away with that for a while if one is lucky or thieving like that child of yours, Stephen, no? Nutrition? Vehicle maintenance, upkeep, etc. Car insurance, too, how about that one? Or those two? One can get away with that one-two (punch maybe) for a while, no? If one is lucky, careful, and skilled, no? Like, very skilled at the art of driving, on wheels, so as not to be soliciting too much unnecessary attention to oneself while driving on the roads, if you will, no? "No deal." Not giving the dogs too many reasons to bite you on the nose, or heel, oh, let's go to the field. What if the brother had reached a point where he had to be doing those types of cutbacks, and was still not able to balance out the books on the fat-cut facts? Therefore, would have seen the need to look further at what else would be there that could be cut back clearly. Then he saw it there in the cup, hot? Yes, it was there, Leigh. He went on to see the possibility of more cuts in the form of tithes and offerings, which he had been paying very faithfully for decades, and often. He thought to himself, "The Lord won't sanction me any further for this, nor the deaf ears of the little miss." Matter of fact, she won't even miss it, nor will the kids that are sitting there on the seats of his... If she does, like, if she misses it, she can easily go sell one or two of the cattle that she has up there on one of the thousands of hills, no? Then, not only would she replace the missing amounts on the bills, but she could also help a brother out, this brother, even. She could help him out with some of the proceeds too, promptly and for oh so many seasons through, couldn't she? "Yes." So, the brother cut it there too. To minimize the risk of being caught with his pants down on the shoe, the brother needs to be less and less in the line of fire. So, the brother took to staying off the road as much as possible, and home on the wire, flirting with "the devil, who, as you already know, is a liar." You know, like, he was staying on the sofa springs, on the bed by her, doing some unholy things somewhere in between, to French fry her. Which was to see him showing up less frequently at those events that you must plan and put in place constantly, he meant. To appease your gods, and the government, and to keep your people occupied. Hence, out of the danger of falling into any troublesome vice, like the little children's pickney dem that they are and therefore, are prone to do; fall into trouble, such as you are, not nice, I know, but... You often see it happening to them via the clearest vision you were given from heaven, in your dreams and your mind. In the visions you had received at her hands, not mine. Yes, your god, and Mums. Or, probably because you know those children may go off and learn the ways of other people, you know them; those foolish heathens amongst whom you now happen to live, and sojourn in a needle. With those very instructions coming from him to rule them, too, and her, Kern. You do this, especially for the sake of those very children. You have surely got to protect them from those heathens' gates. Their ways are not ours, only their money and dates. That's ours, and their other fine things, like cars, which they would have built and created and then used to entice people like us; people like you and me, yes, my star, to come and serve them, perpetually. With the promise to us of getting some, like some of their very fine things, like plumb plums, and more beautiful "Somes," puddings too, maybe. For ourselves, and a bunch of keys, on the shelves lately. That was the promise, real or implied though those promises might have been, to Thomas, Jean, and King, in lies. We came, we saw, and they? They conquered, yes, they conquered us. Didn't they?

Little is much more. Continuing with a few more of the "what-if" things. What if the brother was at the time, having real difficulties, like, dragging the weight along and getting dirty on the knees, while trying to dig himself out of the money pit that he'd found himself in lately, ish? The catchment dams, too, in recent times? "Woo!" "Yuh bit..."

What if the people who were supposed to, and had sworn to help him, along with virtue? What if they were the very ones who were there, busily dragging him down? Or pushing him further into the money-pit round, by their selfish and misguided ways and habits? Some of which (by the looks of things) were being taught and learned right there amongst you in churches circling? By the rabbits' half wings, too, no? Like, in some of those very "well-planned out programmed happenings, right by you? "Probably true." What if that brother had purposed in his heart that he was going to test his God on this one to see if she was smart, by seeing it through, and to its logical ending part? Unlike what he'd come to see, which seemed to be prevalent as the norm among some of you? Yes, me too, and them, amongst all of us, even. Although we profess to be one thing, we practice quite another, to our sin. "Oh, my brother! You mean..." "Yes, that's what I'm in..."

So, "no divorce," you say. "We don't believe in or support it that way." But divorcees are leaders everywhere among you. Some who teach and "preach the word" in your churches, too. Some who've been there to teach you those very things that are now practiced routinely. Including, but not limited to, you and me, Leigh. Teaching us how to behave, or more like, to misbehave. Furthermore, what if the vow the brother had taken and made before the king was a sacred thing, offered up for, and to a holy God, or him, yes, the one who's preaching? What if, just like me, and you, and many of the other leaders, and prominent people there amongst whom... "Yes, you, you..." You who have made those same sorts of vows, and then some among you have gone and broken them? Wow! What if it should turn out that the one true test that God was searching for, and maybe, still is? What if it's to find that one, "someone" who would follow through and honor a vow, mi pickneys?

What would God think now of you and me? What if a part of the struggles the brother was going through at the time was due to some things that he had done? Things that he probably should not have done. No, we're not talking about that one, not those. Not those types of "somethings" here, Batman, now grows... The "thou shalt not" types of gears. But the types like offering up some timely help to someone in need of ecclesiastical gear. Someone like a sister, a brother, or even Steve, the same one who is sitting there and puffing on the weed. "By bailing him out financially?" "Yeah! Said speed." Or was it her? "Oh, yeah, I..."

I heard you, oh, thou shalt not do that either. But my brother! What if? What if you're sitting there smug in the satisfaction of hearing the man say it out loud, that which you already knew all along, and were even thinking about it, and are proud? Yeah! Proud of being among the first to know the same thing as the rest of them. Even at the very moment before he'd said those things, you knew. So now you're here, busily misrepresenting what the brother is saying, and how he thinks, these things through? What if that thing that the brother had done was to bail another brother out of the gutter with some... You know, like, rum? Or a sister? One who was from amongst us and was having a really difficult time financially, to assist her? What if that said party had gone afterward and done the unthinkable? Like, not only did she not pay back the loan that she'd borrowed, and which was drinkable, but that would have been his to do, by him and at his own hands. Yet it was required and payable by the other man. But no, she went along doing a whole myriad of shuffling, trickery, and dishonest wheeling and dealing that seemed to us to serve no purpose other than to trick me, to push the person who'd helped in bailing her out, deeper, deeper in... No, not in the love of Jeezas but, deeper into a hole? What if the brother ended up in a big pile of mess and out of the fold-up fortress, all because of this, that, and the house dress? What if that didn't stop there? What if (among other things) the borrower ended up calling the cops on the lender because the lender had the unmitigated gall to show up at her door in the night? Or more like, early evening to be exact, and precise? What if that visit was to try and get her to do the thing that is right and honorable? Like, based on the fact, not the offering vice from the terrible, but, yes, that, like, to honor the commitments and repay the loan she had borrowed and repent? What if the efforts had failed? What if all of this was made known to the church and its leaders — "And the in-house voicemail readers?"

"Yes, that could work as a breed her..." What if your god in a book somewhere had given instructions as to how to handle such situations? What if those instructions should include taking the matter to you in that very instance, as the brother did do? What if the said church and leadership did absolutely nothing to rectify the said situational grief? No sanction, no suspension, no nothing, nothing at all to bother to mention about the thieves? Well, not quite. What if they did promote the offending party that night? What sort of message would that be sending to onlookers like the "Smartly and Bright..." "Yes." Many of them might have known about some aspects of the "sit you Haitian," beforehand. If not, they could come to know the story later on and make judgment calls on someone, no? What if the lender had decided to go along with it and see where this road also leads the prophets? What if, in the hardest of times, like when he had to stop paying the tithes because he's now a lender-turned-giver and unwise, or more like a debt load underwriter, to be precise? What if he'd decided that this could be seen as his contribution to said cause and purpose on the right side of the circus... sorry, I meant to say, churches, of the churches' parking lot? The tithes cause, even? To the family, like, to the church family, and her courtesies? Would that be just? Could it be justified? What if this, none of it, is hypothetical to the eyes-sis? Could it fit in the purses? Should the brother continue paying those tithes to the deadly call, and his demise as the curse is, first off, after all? (No matter what), just as he'd been doing all those years, and on the lot? "Yeah! Just like you'd said, my pops." Meanwhile, hoping, trusting, praying, and believing, all those things that, believing in them, were what would have served in bringing about this very situation, with him. Should he continue along in the same mode, hoping for some more prayers, wishing for different outcomes today, and going on down the road, liars? No, not this one. But then. Then they go off to church and sing those sweet, melodious songs of yours, again, like. "There's no better way to rob all my brothers" (and sisters too, perhaps). "Than to trust and don't pay," and shop and defray, and freeload the whole way, but never could reach the bay. Or anywhere else worth reaching, I'd say, on this side of the Milky Way. Like, heaven, you say, yours even. Did you know, did it ever occur to you that those aforementioned things, and codes, are sometimes hidden within the game boards? What if these were possible deterrent factors and clothes? Could it be that those were the very things that the brother was wearing, bearing with, and going through at the time, and sinking faster down the sheaves? Believing what you and those others like you have been telling him and bringing him after, the thieves? That would have been the very thing you know, that would have brought him to the current situation that he was to find himself trapped in, at the helping stations below. Like, "Bring the tithes and offerings into the storehouse, and prove me now," you say, and bowed? Oh yeah, I hear you, I know it too. It wasn't you who'd said this, it was the Lord. She would have written it down in the holy words and sent it to us, Ward. "Give, and it shall be given to you, pressed down, shaken together, and running over, too." All of the other used, to the overused positions, scriptures, and texts that you loved so very much to use, and overuse in excess. Above all the other scriptures and the news, I'm vexed. Those are designed to convey a message that, if you do this, then God will do that. Right?

What if, after years and decades of one following that queue, those mantras, and you, one were to wake up one day to realize it ain't working out quite like that, boo? By then, though, you had fallen too deeply in and, under the weight, were beginning to realize that that situation was not, and would never become, sustainable. At least not for you being a mortal person and all, and stainable. Should such a person continue along that self-same path to the fall, unabated? Well, this mocking fool right here, who's feeding the kid the beer, wasn't going to. No matter what anyone says or does to them, too. "While I live," he'd said,

"I'mma gonna keep on seeking and searching out other paths to my bed. Like sensible people sometimes tend to do, and run at it with the fastest shoe, as said. Until that day comes, the day when, per adventure I, even I, might become sensible too, before I die and go off to heaven, with a view on high... and away from you. Until then, though, look at you, a-boo."

8

Chapter eight

Y ou sure know how to Tell Sad Stories, too.
So, because of what would have happened to a songstress or two from somewhere. Those who'd happened to get their early start singing in church all night long, down there, of course, and daytime, too. They then went on to make a name for themselves singing other songs for him and you, other than those they used to sing in churches' long queues. Making a name big enough that everybody everywhere knew it, even you. Just because they did that, they would have managed to reach those meteoric heights. But then, they might have happened to fall like a kite, shush! Then rise and fall again, seven, eight, nine times, ten, and many more times than that, my friends. Just because of those things, every chance you get to point this out, the fall part of those stories as they were coming from the mouths, on chord strings. You do just that, you point out how those people would have fallen flat. But you never once talked about how they'd risen up the charts, all that many times, rising. How about those others who would have traveled along those same paths, but had never fallen so fast, among the thieves, not even once? Or, at least, not so much as to become a headline, on which to feast, as an example of folks who have fallen from grace. So that those other folks, not you, of course, can have them to show and tell to the latter end. Not you, just them, yes, wink and pout at them. They use those as examples to talk about as reasons why other young and gifted people who, from time to time, may rise from amongst you, should do nothing. You'll bombard them with those stories as reasons why they should not even consider

doing anything. Be it great or small, with the great talents that they may now have, or might sometime in the future be found to possess. Lest they too should go the same way; the fall way, I guess, and from the blessing of the day.

Isn't it rather peculiar, though, isn't it curious, that you never seemed to remember to mention those other very talented folks on the bus? Those who would have come up the same way, and would have gone on to make something of their lives? Would have stayed at the top of their game, even to the very end of the knives, making their names. You never bothered to tell their stories to those young and talented folks amongst you, such a shame. One might wonder why, why not? In the meantime, though, you take them and their talents and use them on show every chance you get (or didn't get). For nothing other than a thank-you card and a promise of blessings from the lord, you bet. Which were never to be forthcoming towards... You know, like, towards the payoff of the debt. Until they (those very gifted ones from over on that side of the way) wear out, lose their talent, waste away, and die, in utter poverty. "Oh my!" "Yeah." Gone are they, to the upward way, to heaven, you say, upon the heights. To that other city, pure and bright, such a waste, such a pity, but the beat goes on; boom, boom, boom. Say it isn't so. Say it's not the way it has always been, or go. Come on, bring your strong arguments along, and come, Barrington.

"Don't use your talent for the devil," you say. All the while pointing the finger at the many talents that were to pass through the church and down your way. They then went on to become household names, but some would have fallen on hard times sometimes or passed away. Being careful to mention only the "Fallen on hard times" parts and use those as reasons to support your arguments of sorts, in your sermons. Never pausing for one moment to note that, for something, or someone to fall, that something, or that "someone" person, would have to be at a higher place previously. How did they get there? How high were they? How many times have these individuals risen (or fallen)? Those were never a part of the sermons as given from... well, I beg your pardon. In contrast, though, to your nose, for every one of those, the vast number of others, many more of the same type of folks like those who'd have fallen. There were, in fact, many others who would have done wonders for themselves, on the clocks, to the high end, coming from the very same sorts of background, even, as that. Like those, the Aretha Franklins of the world, the Ray Charles'. Chuck Berry's and the list goes on, on the causes, for Papaya, and Cherry's... But they were never mentioned in your sermons, no, we never mentioned those. Except for when they die, on those occasions, they're likely to get a passing mention from us, in disguise from the mainland. From you, and the likes of you, and with glowing admiration too, ma main man. Who knew? Then there was that other one, the brother man who would not be tamed, the one who was a wild ass of a man, and the blamed. He, too, had hopes and dreams, and a meager getout plan to steam. Talent? Maybe not so much, I mean. He was amongst you, though, and crushed. He'd set out on a mission to do some things and grow, thought it would be good to make it known to you, like so, you know, in the sense of community, the spirit of togetherness, you see. We rise and fall together, right? Yes, preferably the rising part tonight, since there ain't much further falling space left for the likes of us and in your faces and sight, seeing on the bus. Some of us know it, but you don't. So, he told you what he was thinking of doing to try to progress ahead of shoe-shining; two counts. "No," you'd said, like always before, mi bred. Because that's the only word you and yours seemed to be familiar with, when it comes to these things and the causes, no, sit. Yes, that's what you'd said, miss, "No," to the young man. Your reasons were many, varied, and quick in coming at hand, to get buried. But this wild ass of a young man was not to be deterred by that. So, he went out and did what he had to do, and then came the fallouts, coming from who? Them, no doubt, and now? Come, come over here and look at this.

While seagulls are in the valley, bickering over droppings of blood and fatty tissue. The eagle is mounting up, going, going, gone, up with the carcass, and eyeing the catastrophe issue which is about to unfold in the form of an avalanche bearing down on them, in the valley, about to swallow them up, and cover them on the trolley, missus. I know, an avalanche may not be such a great threat to seagulls in a valley, with you. "Seagulls have wings," you say, they'll mount up and fly away, and out of alms' way. Yes, I know that much. But what if we're not here talking about those kinds of see gullibles, I mean, seagulls, sorry. What if we're talking about something else, far away from here, on the belts and terrible? "Oh, Christ's, Sis." "I know, but..." What if the eagle has other reasons for not making the seagulls any wiser, be it about the avalanche, the pending danger, or anything else for that matter, for us to go out and eye-stare her, stranger? What if it all fits perfectly well into the schemes and plans of that self-same eagle and the man? After all, if all the seagulls are gone, there will be one less enemy for him to storm. Yes, one less competition for him to worry about, Mom, and perhaps, much more spoil for the taking of that eagle, and for feeding the mouths of Pops, Mon, and the weevil. Wouldn't there be? Just asking, you see! I'm allowed to ask, am I not?

...

"Red," you say, they are, like, red something, or another car. From the head top down to the shoulder scar. But they'll be something before they're older, by far. That man and his brother, though, no, not the other. But as for me, and you? Holy Father! "Ooh-ee." Your male folks compared muscle to strength and might, and never managed to get anything right, except for the few here and there, of course. Your female folks? They show off their bodies and shapes, with nothing between their ears, and nothing but nonsense gets to escape through those very ears and noses. Except for the few here too — "And fragrance from Rose Sis?" "True." Guess where those few end up? Yep, over there serving the other guy, boo, bringing in the teacup, oh my! Yeah! To the same one you'd said was weak, and who you still thought about as recently as this past week, especially at the end of the week. You like to boast too; always boasting about how he's inferior and too sweet for you. But they, too, (our successful few)? They are busily helping him to build his country, aren't they? Just the same as you, and me, yay, all of us. We're all here building this strong country, his fortified cities, his mighty armies, some of them can be found right there, yes, arming you. Those armies of theirs are based over there on your... I mean, on our little piece of ground, on the square. Or on what should have been so, our piece of ground, so I hear. But while you were there, standing over him and flexing your very strong muscles around his skin, and such. He was applying himself to gain knowledge and understanding of sound. (Don't touch). Technical know-how, too, and commanding... He's now running all over necks, and you and your kind of kings stand too, and you don't even know enough to have known that much. He's sending men to the moon and beyond, and you? As for your god, or your myriads of gods, and moms, wow. Oh, how mad she must be; she's surely going to be angry at me when you're done reading this, if you ask me. Ask none rod, I mean Nimrod, ask Nimrod again, he'll tell you, my friend. This leads me to the next question at the day's end. Or to ask it again, since I might have asked it already somewhere else, on all the ends. How and when did these people (my people)? How and when did we get to become so comfortable in our misery, so much so that we've forgotten that we are miserable, and how to be mean? How did we allow ourselves to be manipulated into such a state as this, and unclean?

Husbands and fathers become irrelevant in the homes and the lives of our children, at someone else's behest and to thrill them. While it's "the government" that now provides for the family, our women say, Wow, yes! This is good, this is very good for me, and I said, No, and they said to me. "Go," while they were pointing a finger to show me the doe, as if it were standing beside me in the doorway. Because you, they said, you don't even know nuttn, not anything, now go away. So, I had to leave among them and go that very day, just like she'd said.

"No," I'd said, it's not that good, it's a continuation of the big scheme, designed and signed in for those fools. Some women can never seem to see through it or understand the tools, and we men nowadays? We don't allow ourselves to live and suffer long enough to get to the point of understanding tough things, either. Like, the rough and the meager. So, these people will remain as the servant class forever, or until we one day wake up and find that we are dead. Yeah, go on, mi bred, scratch your head, and laugh as much as you like. Or wake up now, this very moment in the night. Start smelling the coffee before that day comes upon you... in it, and bright. But wait a minute, it already might, like, it might have. But, but, but these people have settled in and will not be moved. "Whatever you do," they have said, "don't wake me up, don't shake me up." Don't disturb my second coffee cup while I slumber. Don't deprive me of my well-earned comfort, "Boy, I really love that number." "I know, but..." Nor outsize me from my well-deserved nervous breakdown, I've worked hard for it, I deserve it, and I won't be let down. I won't have you, or anyone else, depriving me of it, thank you very much, and sit, go over there and sit down. So, go on stroking your funny bone, all night long. Sing the swan song, and go rest at home, sleeping in a little piece of heavenly peace. Nothing hard for you, none of these. Not even hard enough to hurt your feelings, oh please. Nor to wake you out of your slumbering, in the cradle up there on the treetop, Humble Lyn. Rock-a-bye baby rock, enjoy the ride tumbling down, don't worry about a thing, sure, not a sudden stop, hitting the ground.

Covenant-breakers, it would seem to me, don't get very far with God to be. However, one must be wise enough to know when a yoke has been broken and not go on re-yoking oneself by replacing the yoke that has been broken. Especially, not with the same broken yoke that was broken. Certainly not by the same yoking yoker who'd yoked you before. When you're free, stay free, take it from me.

"Don't overthink it," I hear someone say. "Or was it, 'You're not here to think,'" as said by another one that day? "You're here to take and follow instructions and to do it 'my way.'" What they're really saying and doing in effect here is conditioning you and your mind not to think about anything but beer, to take leave of your senses. Just obey and do as they say; follow instructions (their instructions) to the "us-ward way." Suit them fine, one might think and speak as if to say... And you, what do you do? You go right along with it to your hurt, then pass it along to the next generation after you, to their hurt, too. Young men, get to know their ways, and know the ways of your women too, in your day. While you're at it, don't let them drain you and your family of all your substances and resources, either of the two. Nor the other precious ones either, as this is. If you let them, they will, and then, they will blame it all on you, Freda. Yes, it will be all your fault, especially if and when you're on the verge of breakthroughs of sorts. Like, when you're on the eve of something big, way up north. Suddenly, they'll be there, armed and ready to make it known to everyone, everywhere, just how undeserving you are for such high callings in the sky, and the silver forks on the wing, and waiting to fly through the air. Anyone can be so inclined, but our women folks are mostly so, as the records will show to Kelvin Clime. Especially "church women," they'll drag you in and wind you up, and when they're done with their blinking eye-deals and the fun in the cup-cup. It will be all your fault, my son. I could tell you stories that will make you get a sudden rush of the shakes, laughing and all, at the dressing on the cakes. But what would that be saying about me in this case? Hardly anything that hasn't been said before, and I'm still here behind the jail E-door and shoving things in your face some more. So, beat it, then heat it, don't you let me repeat it anymore. But then again, it's probably okay for one to ask some questions and quickly send them off to them with things to say. So, I will do just that, I will ask you this, Mr. Matts, right away. What will that be saying about me, really? Hmm, hmm. Too trusting, too gullible, too doggish? Perhaps all three... are inedible. Or this; maybe I'm just a man trying to survive the new world of the dominant woman, come-lately. Like her there, and your girl over here, not me. Why is it happening like that anyway? Who is sitting there planning and scheming these things in the play? Why, what's the ultimate objective here? Oh my. I have my suspicions, but then again. Beware of them, don't cry.

...

Easy street, look at it. Easy Street might not be so easy after all, but *mek weh dweet,* because ease is what you like best. Come to think of it? We all like things that way — "Undressed?"

"No, I meant to say, all-dressed and easy, aren't we?"

"Yes." But if I wore you (as a dress, perhaps), but no, I meant to say, Were. If I were you, I'd get off that street and fast. When I was you, I did just that, I'd gotten up off that street. But not before I would have managed to figure out some things for myself, while caring for the meek. I'd started to wander around their shelves for something to eat, and asked; What if... What if the easy way is not such a good thing for Fonda, and May, not a good way after all, down yonder? "O — kay!" What if the hard way is the better way out, from the fall, and dunked under? What if someone, somewhere, is busily manipulating the system to get some folks over here... folks like us, for instance, my dear? For the most part, not necessarily us, though, just those other folks of sorts who may be said to be looking remotely like us when seen through the peephole above the door corks. What if that same someone was there, busily trying to get them to think that they've arrived? Life is easy now, nothing to worry about anymore, when there, in fact, are many great reasons for us to worry? What if he, that man, just like me, everyone else, and Sam... you well, Curry? Yes, just like every other man everywhere. What if he's there, busily positioning himself in the best place to be able to get others to serve him, in the square? To go out and work for him for a tiny fraction of the real value of the work that he did, for him. When he's done working for the little morsel that he pays him, and you. You gleefully ran out to the nearest shopping mall, or even the faraway one, and tall. His shopping malls are... yes, they all are his, but you didn't know or consider those things. They're much too small for your earrings that were their ringing the hearing on and off the herrings, and you? You just wanna go shopping. Or more like, playing your favorite sporting game; shopping, who's asking? "Me."

"But of course." Giving back that little morsel you'd just received from the hands of the thieving parson, and him. You go giving it back to the same person who'd just given it to you, to sling. You give it all back in exchange for next to nothing, that which he'd just given to you in the form of a paycheck. Watch the "check" part of the word around that neck. It's probably a checker marker, no less. Not from the lord and to light up the spark yet, but the one that he has to perform. But only because he was forced to do so as a front lawn. Showing off to you and those other ones who are peeping through the door screw... hole, that things are changing for the better, man. When, in fact, if they're changing at all, they're changing for the worse for you and the nedda E-on... me, to crawl. Others like you and me, too, and Paul. Meanwhile, we sang the swan songs, sorry, I meant to say, the sweet songs. We sing sweet songs and dance, while the piper plays another familiar song all day long, luring us down to our ultimate doom. But ease is what we, like beasts... sorry, I meant to say, best. Yes. We like things that are easy and undressed. So, we choose the easy way out, the easy street way, no doubt. "We all sometimes do, no?" "Yes." We surround ourselves with people who can help us get along. Help us out of the rut whenever times are bad, and everything's going wrong with us, and the chorus, mi gad. People such as families and friends, dads, too, and moms. If and when we find out that we don't have much of those kinds to defend, we create some for ourselves or join up with the already established dens. Those well-accepted groups are there on the ends, too. Such as churches and their many auxiliary groups, Sis, with an "amen." For instance, just for instance. Then all of a sudden, wild strangers were to become our sisters and brothers, not cousins, though, but still... all this to the hurt and alienation of our real sisters and brothers, go. Just because the real ones may be a bit far off, too far from reach at the present moment, of course. More than a car trip away, perhaps, and from the torments in the nests of rats. But the adopted ones are always close at hand. Or more often than not, they are still there when we call on them, and vice versa, swap. But what do I know about such? Nothing, what pile of craftiness anyway? Now, go sing, go away. No, I know you won't go, because you need to hear what else I've got to say.

Be careful how you go about bailing people out of their perceived predicaments. You might be doing them (as well as yourself) more harm than good in so doing; that's what he meant. If you want to help someone out, then do it through a charitable organization or a welfare plan, of sorts, never on a one-on-one basis, no hand-to-mouth. There are lessons in each of life's experiences that one may need to learn, if one is to be going anywhere worthwhile, in this life or on the spaceship to turn, the show in... But if we were to cut the experience short, we might be found to be "depriving" those said "someone" of valuable lessons of sorts. Lessons that they were not given enough time to learn from, and the opportunity to suffer enough through and earn some. To mature properly and grow a ton, to reach their full potential, even if slowly. It's okay to help a person out sometimes or help them up whenever they fall down the mines, mi pickney. But you need to know when to stop, for both your sakes and the homes on the lots. So, the adopted ones, the adopted families in these and such other plans, may take on much more immediate importance than the real ones. Because the real ones are far away, and will likely cause you some hardships at times, like, even today, if and when they happen to be close at hand. Like, if and when you're close up with them, the real ones. That is because that's the thing with "real." Sometimes "real" can be a bit heavy, like steel. The adopted ones, though, are not so. They are like a present that helps in times of trouble, and while "slow" is heavy on the go. Or so it might have seemed, to Cleo. The adopted ones, that you always seem to have anyway, are the real trouble, but you wouldn't know, okay? So, it's much better to stick with the fake or adopted ones than the real ones, because the adopted ones are near, always, right? Is this the best way in the long run, though, and into the night? Couldn't you be there, placing far greater importance on insurance than on building wealth, to spearhead their... Real wealth, that's right. The real family wealth kind that, if you have enough of, you probably won't need so much insurance props. A little yes, for prudence's sake perhaps, and best, for your endurance along the winding tracks. But not for your only hope of salvation in this life to see, in the long run, away from me, in the real scheme of things, and good fun e-rats. Don't despise those friends and them (our adopted families), no. They do have their real values and places to go. I've had some great ones in my life and in my time; friends that are like that, yeah! Like a fine wine, people who were there for me in the rough times.

"I can't thank you enough, nor can I be ungrateful to you for what you've done for me in my hours of need, which were many and tough. The evil one wanted me to hate you, tried very hard to do that, too, but I couldn't, I can't, I won't."

But I was made to realize that I was doing my best friends an injustice in an oversized apron props; a continuation of the scheme to our fix in disguise, perhaps. Or so it seemed to me, guys. The help that my friends had offered me had to come from somewhere for a fee. Someone had to do without or go without something, even for a brief moment in time. Even a brief moment of time. It was taken from somewhere else and afforded to me like limes, so that I could get the help that I needed from my friends. I also came to discover that no help that came to me from anyone, or from anywhere, comes without a cost, and dare, it's a cost that is going to have to be repaid, one way or another, one day or the other. Even if you don't pay back directly the person from whom you'd gotten the help of the loan in the first place, as is often the case in this race. You're going to be made to pay. For example, you will find it very hard to say "No" to the next person who asks for your help. Especially if and when you can help, or think you can, and there again is where your wake-up call may lie, helpless in the pan. When you're there thinking you can help, when in fact, you can't. "Tell me about it."

"No, Aunt, I won't."

"Well, no. Don't bother to tell me, one dunce... I already know, by experience and all, the other counts."

"I know, I know much more about that type than any one person should ever have gotten to know in one lifetime and heading towards the fall."

Chapter nine

Seek, and You Shall Find a Job

There are some folks in whose houses and business establishments our women folks often end up finding that "job" we'd been praying and seeking our gods for, because we wanted so very much to have it, and the car. Our female folks are the chief culprits here. Those folks, though, of our "employer kind," can and will do some great things. They've been teaching us many things, inadvertently though it might have been, that we badly need to learn. But learning was never our forte, nor our concern. So we come away from there, skinning the beast and grinning our shiny white teeth at finding all sorts of things to mock and say. Things to laugh at and talk down about these very folks all day, instead of learning the lessons right away. Then, we end up in church testifying and glorying in our well-rehearsed words, craftily designed to ridicule those same folks, well, so I heard. But we all know how such things go. "Fools," they say, "make a mockery of sin." I even heard you saying so, ever so often. The only mocking fool to be found anywhere, though, as records will (without fail) show, is us. Yes, you and I, on the bus, just to get things in the proper perspective here for everyone to see and get riled up at it and cuss. All of us together as a people are the laughingstock of the entire modern world and are even being set up for extinction, not for the new boyfriend or the girl, but we don't even seem to know it. We don't take such things to heart. We never bothered to take anything to heart, except for heaven, perhaps; we just want to go there. But why should anyone save people like us? Why should anyone care? What value is there in doing so? Is there any worth in saving the likes of us and those, as is...? Does your god even care? Should she? Yeah, go ahead, laugh at me, and argue about that too, you've got no lack in those regards, Sue, arguing. Go now. Do a Google search on the term "Sustainable population growth." Same as I did when I started the search. Be sure to take the time necessary to read through the results. See if there may be any cause for concern here, as it applies to people like you and me, my dear. Google it up, Google it up, Google it up, and read along now. There's a bunch of information on those pages if you scroll down. They said the earth, as it now is, can sustain only the Europeans, in other words, only that size population. "Coincidence or what?"

"What!" Where does that leave the rest of the people like us, all of them and us, those who're out there now riding on the idling bus?"

"Mi nuh nuo, but. We're going to have to do something about it," they said. What "we?" Who are the "We" of whom they speak and refer to in the results? What "something" are they thinking of doing as it occurs? Will it be overt or covert? Where will it lead the reparation crew to leave the rest of the people of the earth, and you? Anyway, what can I say? You go right on, continue the same as you've often done; pray. No doubt, you'll be okay. Or you can get up off that thing and start doing some other things, in a few other new ways. Don't forget, though, the robots are coming, so go. Buy our kind of things from our kind of people, even if it costs a bit more coming to us out of the vehicle, it is better than buying plastic at the other guy's store.

"Can you dig it some more?"

"Yes, I can, I planted it, remember that one, Phillip?"

"Yes, but..." If we're ever going to get anywhere worth being in this present life, we need to start thinking about some silly little things and insights. Ask some nonsensical questions too, such as these: What is it that is worth having, in this life? Worth working for, worth spending money on, worth saving money towards, etc. However, those things are for sissies; they're not for us, not for people like you and me, Chrissy, we're not pigmies in the circus. No, don't cuss. We're big people, strong and mighty, so why bother? If we don't know these things, though, my little brother, we'll never get away from depending on the other. The other people's things, yes, and it's obvious that we as a people don't, nor will we bother to count them. We're not going anywhere, and fast, as an individual or as a person, in class, trying to count to ten. Or, if by some weird, calculated arguments, we're said to be going somewhere towards the home ends? We would probably be found to be going in the wrong direction from there, towards more torment. Or even worse. Headlong down the road where someone else is busily pushing us, towards our curse of carrying the loads. Even unto extinction, and the chorus, of course, go on now, cuss. But, unbeknownst to us, while we were there, we were busy praying, singing sweet songs about beautiful nothings, and swaying, dancing away, even. Our very survival was leaving. But what in the healing stream does this fool know about him anyway? Good evening, Miss Faye. Robots are coming, too, okay?

Who wants to argue with my view on these things? Who wants to debate? Come sometime around eight. Bring your strong arguments and some coffee beans on the plates. Bring on some more "some" too, and your soul-saving faiths, bring your evidence and supporting facts. While you're at it, in all of your bringing in of those sheaves and things, be sure to bring proof that you don't have ulterior motives for your opposite stance on the matter, like, on these truths and things. Could the status quo be more to your liking, my brother? Could that be the reason why you're on that side of the argument and the border? Just asking. Am I allowed to ask him?

...

Picking up attitudes and other such things. The story is told about one who was seen doing a crossword puzzle. Halfway through the puzzle, she came across a four-letter word to muzzle. The given clues said something that is usually found at the bottom of the pigeon coop. (Or even at the bottom of it, in truth, yes, a chicken coop). It could be found there too, but oops. The last two letters were already in the four-letter word slot. Those were the letters "i" and "t." "Easy like that, you see."

She said this to herself, not me, while filling in the slots and continuing along with the rest of the puzzle, to please me. Somewhere near the finishing point of the puzzle, though, she ran smack dab into a problem on the slow go, no? "Yes." Something was wrong because, try as she may, she couldn't find the right words to properly fill in the remaining blocks that day. But upon some quick revisions, she was to find that everything fits like a hand-in-glove when she'd inserted "g, and r," with lots of love, into those slots in front of the "i," and the "t," as said above. That was, after she was done erasing and replacing the "g" and the "r" where "s" and "h" were inserted in their respective places. Of course, both words seemed to fit perfectly well into the slot and the given clues. But one is correct, which means the other is not. One was the right answer, the other was, in fact, wrong, Sir. One is soft, malleable, even; the other is rough and tumble, and can be durable too. One is tender and cushy; the other is hard and coarse. More or less like some of us are, of course. Yeah! That would be us. This motley fool, even, and the chorus. The soft one, anything soft, can seem so very attractive to the class, lovable to some, perhaps. Apparently, easy to work with, inviting, and friendly. The hard ones, though, not so much so, with Hensley. One may add a little soft powder to the hard one and throw in bits and pieces of strong metals, such as steel here and there, add water and mix well, and one could build something as strong and durable as... well. Like, something that will be able to last for decades, centuries, even. What can one do with the other mushy stuff? Not very much, so stay away from it, or you might wake up somewhere down the road ten thousand years from now to find the overload, like, finding out that you're still full of ...it. Yes, man. Still full of that soft, mushy pot of she... If one, under those same circumstances, should somehow manage to live and survive that long, sis. So, of those two things that are sitting there at the bottom of the pigeon coop, which one do you want when you reach in there for the poop... No, leave it (as is) and go, boo. Get something while you're in there, though, whatever you do, do get something. Then get your as... assumptions and bits and pieces out again. Pieces such as your arms and length, with that other piece. Well, if you had stuck it in there too, for long, like this. Long time nuh see yuh, "buddy." Let's go to the feast, cuddly. Whatever "it" is, though, get it back out of there and get on with the business of life, living with what you'd fished out when you'd reached in that night.

I became aware of some things early in my life. Well, early is relative here, so let's say earlier; earlier than most other folks, or a certain kind of "other folks" warming themselves there by the fire and the smokes. I quickly learned some things, and that was why I stuck it out this long with him. I had to get one of those things from among the things that were there at the bottom of the pigeon coop. I saw them there when I was tossed in (or was it me who had jumped in)? I don't even know for sure, my home friend. Whatever the case might have been, though, I was there, I saw them below, and I knew which one I wanted. I took hold of the hard one, the most difficult one in the ordeal. The one that most, if not all, of the others who had gone in there didn't want. They were quick to dismiss it from under the plant. But as for me? I took hold of the hard one and stuck it out this long. See? No regrets so far, my star. Well, a little bit of that type, maybe, on the roads of hot tar; a few of the "regrets" here and there, yes. But not enough for me to write home about, my dear, at the old address. Well, I guess... It doesn't matter much to me anymore, though, like, what people might say, how they feel about me, or even how they play. How much they may try to disenfranchise me, get back at me, mock me, or spill me. If only I got a chance to do what I was born to do or was called to do in the evening (curfew). I'm a winner after all. We're all alike after all this, in a few ways, and this right here is one of the surest of the few upon which to gaze, over beers. We all will die, so death to me is not revenge; it's not vengeance, or even settling of the accounts with them. It's not because I did (or didn't do) those things that's why I died. If that is the case, then why are you dead? Because even though you don't know it in your head, yet, that's where you are, mi bred, go fret, because you're already dead. What have you done with your life that you can even hope to leave here on this earth to live on after you, like, after you're done gone too? Shouldn't that be the thing for you to be thinking of above all else, and to focus on, mostly? Or is it? What do I know? Oh, sheet! Just asking, Bro. Beausey.

10

Chapter ten

Pastors Know What's Best. Yes?

You know them, pastors and friends. Pastors are God's spokespersons here on earth, so they say; therefore, you must listen to them and obey. If they say "go," you go; if they say come, you come because they know the way, and you don't, okay? If they say do this, you do it, because they know how things are done, and you don't know a thing. They have a direct line to the crater, you know, like, to the creator and maker of all things greater, or even the lesser ones, but you don't. I've seen many of them, and at the end of the day, one is left to wonder, really wonder about some things. About them, even. How is it that some of these pastors and friends seem to have so much trouble getting anywhere, or getting anything done out there, without the aid and assistance of other folks, other seemingly lesser folks than themselves? Yet they, yes, they again, are the ones who are going to show me the way to heaven. Telling me how to go about getting there with them, like, if I even want to go there, like they say I should. Or is he trying to make me believe that I ought to, like, want to, want to go there? Go where? In there, in there, Kojak in there. Yeah! Sometimes people *haffi tek bad sinting mek laugh*, so I was able to hear it in their multitude of talks. "Why?" Because of this, too, if you never knew the news, it's not for you, that's why. Yes, you.

Did you come from there, though? Heaven, did you come from there? "No?" Well, you sure ain't going. What did the Bible have to say about that, Joe Hingh? The next time you happen to hear them reading your favorite scripture verse. Yeah, that one coming out of their hands, first; for God so loved the world... tell them to return three verses to St. John 3:13. Start there and learn what it says on that subject to work in. Do you still want to go? No?

Then come those traveling salespersons; pastors, as they are sometimes called, and worse than... Yeah, for your laughter, I'm certain, and for the altar call. Preachers too, evangelists, prophets, and such the likes as that — "Who's it, mass Fitz?" "No, not him, but..." The Lord had sent them to you and me. She'd sent them to preach and teach in your churches, to bless you and anoint you, and your purses. To tell you lies and... Sorry, I meant to say, to open up your eyes to what the Lord has got in store for you, in the church and way up there in your mansion in the skies, clear and blue. So, they stood you up in long lines in front of an altar. Pours oil on your head and flies in your Malt Sir, *yes sah, same way mi sey, sah*! Anoints you from your right ear down to your right great toe. Leaving the wrong one in your shoes and socks on the floor and coming out on the right side of your fortune too, too fast towards our... Then they send you out on the mission field that she sees afar off. Somewhere in your future, where you never end up going or reaching anyway, to salute her horse. Everyone in the line was told what everybody already knew. It was true, the fact that these great and mighty people have got great places to go and marvelous things to do do, don't do... All in the name of, guess who? Yes, and to the glory of the lord, that's who. There were none of the other types of folks there in that long line, though. Nor hanging from the strand on the card for a long time, go. Like, those who were going to become roadkill or the victims of some violent actions, of sorts, then come to their demise, still. Or those who go somewhere else, like, gone all the way downhill — "To health?"

"No." To a place where we all know that they, yes, those other people and their children are going to go anyway. Although any and everyone could have prophesied this and told them so, you know. Like, tell them where they're going to go; those other people, like John, Jean, and Shane Doe. They're going to prison, jails, and even death row. But as for those kinds? They weren't there at the time, no. Those kinds of people are from families who, to church, they never go. So, they only got what was coming to them anyway, no? In the meantime, though, the preacher performed wonders there on the "church flow." As in, the floor. In every aisle and the many rows, just as before. But the preacher had to move on now; he had to take the Godspell to those other people somehow. Sorry, I meant to say, the gospel, okay, sorry again, Ms. Faye. Therefore, he will need to pick up, pack up, leave, and go. No, it's not because "he doesn't love you no Moe," as in, anymore, it's not that, I'm sure. But it's because the preacher has got to take the great message and burden of the cross that he carries for the people of ours at last, to them. These kinds of marvelous people, of course, amen. Some are still out there in some other pastures fair and have not yet heard those kinds of wonderful words of theirs. Those that he and he alone had received at the mouth of the Lord, beware. "You bet." He must go and give it to those other people, too, before he moves on and out, and away from you. But before he walks back out through the door, his pocket will be a lot heavier than before. Because you would have given up your last pinch of dough, even though you've not paid back the loan that you'd borrowed it out of and taken it from, and which you still owe the man at the exchange post, of the program. But there's no need for you to worry, no, that's for the show, I mean, for sure, that's for sure. Because the blessings are coming soon, pressed down and shaken to overflow (the moon). "Go on now, go back to church, no?"

"No, not to church this time, but worse."

"I know, I know." Go to the other happy place over there near the signpost to post on social media and such, and bow-string the chorus too, well, of course, my friends, yes, it's true. Like, take it to social media again, let them lie to you there, too, or tell you the truth, the naked truth, even. Just one more thing, though, before I, too, have to leave and go. Why is it that the prophecy thing and the "real" reality thing don't seem to add up ever, for this morbidly over-churched bunch and the clever? Mere bad luck? Good luck on that one; the bad luck bit, yes, man, and on the yawn.

...

Got a bone to pick here with a pastor, my dear. Yes, your pastor, right there. She who is there serving in your church, and after that, like. After we're done this evening, she'll most likely be there, still. But as of now, go ask her about it, she'll answer your queries, and quickly, I swear, she will. Go on, take a look and see, she's right there this very moment, well, probably. Or was it he, like, him, maybe? Anyway, back to it. Yes, it has everything to do with something I saw at the wedding there at the church last weekend. Yeah, I was there to meet them. Well, no, I wasn't even supposed to be there, but hear this, friend. My son was gigging with the backing band, and he wanted me to accompany him going along. For moral support, you know. My son and I have always been tight like that, of course, yes, I'm his beloved pops. Anyway, I just couldn't believe what I saw there, my eyes almost popped out of the socket at the stare. A fifty-member bridal party and to spare, can you believe that? No, oh no, don't you get me wrong here, I agree, a person can do whatever she wants Ted to do, sorry, I meant to say, wanted —
"To do, do, and see?"

"Yes." Those people can too; it's their day. I have no problem with them that way, well, perhaps a little bit, but... My big beef here is not so much with them, but with the pastor again, of course, your pastor, even, yeah, that sort, Steven. How could she stand there and preside over a setting like that? Not just any old setting but a wedding, white frack, how could she? Think of it for a moment, like me. If you know me well enough (and I think you do by now), I have been saying some things for quite a long while, lots of things, like, wow! Things that I have no business saying, some have said. Some of those sayings of mine got me into a lot of hot water with the bred, and some other folks that way, even while I was praying for them one day.

"Like what?"

"My chat." Like my views on the number of our young people who are sitting in our churches just wasting away, in decay. Becoming old people before they even knew it, I'd say. Before they even get a chance at living, and watching their time and chances slip away. At least, I am sitting and watching these things, and seeing it happening before my eyes, knees deep within the prayer cloth. While they (for the most part) seemed to be thinking that they still had lots of time to make a slow start. That their prince and princesses will soon be coming online, in a go-kart. Coming in to get them skinned, riding in on white horses, even. So delusional. Yes! Oh yes, my original, friend. It has everything to do with it, everything. Ask any of these young people why they're not married yet, ask them who, or what they are waiting on, or even for, like, what are they waiting for to get married? Ask them about it and see what they tell you. I'm grieved. Matter of fact, I have, I've asked several of them, on many occasions too, although the answers were many and varied coming through. It has always come down to one key constant, and that is this: at the end of the day, they're still sitting there waiting on the kids, aunt's friend. Waiting and wasting away, grating the nutmeg, Meg. As for the answers I get from them to those questions of mine. It's always like "I'm not ready for that yet, I can't find a good man (or woman), I can't afford it right now," and the list goes on somehow. But right there, at the "I can't afford it" part, is where I have an issue with these pastors, of sorts. This particular pastor at this latest wedding gig, as a matter of fact, ole Far... Many of her very own members were sitting there all dressed. Some were participating in the acts, or playing support roles, more or less. Yes, most likely. But they were there too, yes, whatever the reason was, they were nonetheless there. Well-dressed, watching, and seeing the same things as I was able to see and saw Hingh, I guess. One member of the bridal party after another marching up, up, up, up, up. It was like, like there was no end to it, not getting to the stop, not even to spit. Just as one begins to think that this is the end, then comes yet another bunch of them. Overdressed, overly decked out in fine, fabulous apparel, and nix-nax, of mine, people. I would have counted as many as forty-eight by the time I realized that something unique and unusual was going on at the gate. That was when I had to stop and restart the counting, a mistake. So, add that to the bride and groom, and you will have around fifty as the amount on the cake in the room. It could have been more, too. Yeah, I'm coming to that, and you. What the pastor has to do with it is this. She already has a whole bunch of people in the church, whose time came and went, and worse, worse than that is this: They didn't even know when it came, God-sent, even. They don't know that it's passed and gone, and there are a whole bunch of younger ones standing at the doors that are ripe and ready already for the picking, some more, sitting there in the pan behind those right now and waiting to score. No, don't yawn. Yet another bunch is coming up fast on their heels. Those who are likely to be coming to face the same fate as these in the ordeal, yeah! For real. All of these young folks have a myriad of obstacles going against them and their hopes, dreams, plans, aspirations, and all their earthly desires already, as they are, out of demand. Real or imagined. But obstacles they are anyway. Now, though, she has gone right ahead and added yet another to the list on this day. I'll tell you what it is. It's the precedent that is now set, by this single misguided action, and yes. It's the act of officiating at a wedding in her very own church, with so many of her own young and unmarried members looking on at the curse, no, I meant to say, at that beautiful one coming in through the doors. A wedding that displayed a fifty-member bridal party. I'm willing to bet that no one among them owns a bridal boutique, or a shoe store like these for your feet, not even a pastry shop, or any such enterprise like that. A tiny restaurant on the corner lot, perhaps. But none with the capacity to accommodate the size of a wedding ball (or bat), such as that. Let alone a party this big and haughty, in their ballroom, swap. From now on, though, every time one of those young people even so much as hears the word "marriage," or "wedding." They will more than likely be thinking, "I can't afford that; I can't afford ma bedding, let alone a wedding." For sure, they (for the most part) won't be able to afford a wedding like that one. But thanks be to God and this big right plan, there are other types of those things, like weddings, which, if only they were made aware of, they would have been able to afford them, *snitch*. More than "afford them," even.

There's this show that I used to love to watch on TV. It consists of a bunch of bearded brutes, like — "Like you?"

"No, not me." Pardon the term here, guys, it's nothing against you, I still love you, loads. But there's this one episode of the show that stood out in my mind and my memory, on these roads. Probably because of the subject matter it was addressing to me, in the code. A subject matter that, as you can see, is my pet peeve, or is becoming one of my pet peeves. In this particular episode, there was a surprise, a big surprise if ever there was one. All the family members: a brother, children, grandchildren, uncles, and aunts. Along with various spouses (where applicable to the plans). Came together and planned a wedding for the matriarch and patriarch of the family. They (Mom and Dad) did not have a big wedding when they got married, yes, to me. Because they were young and probably penniless at the time, as it was, see? "Yes." But not so anymore, though, they got it done and went on with the business of living, and living was what they did, in fine style and occupying the crib in... They would have raised a fine handful (or two) of children of their own, and so, they are now at the "sit-back-and-relax stage of their lives." Comfortable in their own home, and working with the forks and knives. The cooking pots and pans, too, are cutting against the bones, and you, no? "No." The officiating minister at the wedding was one of their very own sons. Whilst the guests (a whole bunch of them, yes, almost to the last person) were family. Their own family. Children and grandchildren, for the most part, were there to handle me. Now, answer me, and compare. Compare this to that type of nonsense that has become prevalent and pervasive in our churches and amongst "our" people, over here, Sis. That which seemed to suggest that marriage, sex, and children are accursed things and are to be avoided at all costs, to him, in our vehicle (I'm vexed), so it would have seemed. If and when they do eventually have one, like a wedding, it has got to cost an arm and a leg in... That is the way of the lord, as far as these people here are concerned, and as they'd wink in accord. The very same "lord" whom (we're told) would have said: be fruitful and multiply and replenish the earth. But we all know the truth that she never said any such thing, as it is accursed. She couldn't and wouldn't have said such nasty and outrageous things to us, and for us who love him, and like, like, so very much. Even worse, that's why she never did, she never said any such thing, to those kids. So, let it be known that we're never going to even so much as venture anywhere near those forbidden things. Our god is depending on us to stay faithful to this cause, and not to sin. "Whatever the cost." But then again, given a choice between these two separate approaches to the matter, and life in general, my friends, and my brother (the original). I will take the way of the bearded brutes on any given day down the shoots. Yeah, you know me like that, yes, that way, and then again.

The pastor was at it again yesterday. Preaching about the fishing dis-ciples in his sermon, and baking cakes. Of course, the focus was on Jesus, who'd escaped the grave's... He was focusing on how one can be looking at him, and talking to him, yes, Jesus, and not even know that it's him. But as for me, I was about to see some other things there, among them, in the very sermon that he was there preaching. So, I'd say, go a-fishing anyway, because "fishers" is what you are, of men, even. So, when catch-ing time comes, it will be fishers who'll be getting some because they'll be in the position to catch fish and reap. Possibly you and me, too, yes, my peeps. You'll know what to do with your catch of fish; you're a fisherman too, like these. You will know who to turn to for a fisher-man's type of help when your nets start breaking under the weight, and what to ditch her on near the shelf of the Apes. You're a fisherman (or woman). So, yes, you will know. You'll have a market ready and wait-ing for your merchandise; you're a fisher. Now take this advice. Go on out fishing, fisherman, no matter what? Let all others sit around and wait and watch the Gold Cup match, in comparison to waiting for Jesus to come to feed them with roast fish and bread on a plate (or cake, on rocks).

When Jesus comes, you see, he approached fishermen, like these. Fishers who've been fishing, but who might have caught no fish, "yet." After Jesus was done with fixing them up good and proper, though, the fishers had fish aplenty to show. What if "non-fishers" had gone out fishing too? Good question, coming from you. Are you a fisherman? Is your storage full now, as it is, and moving on? Is your net already full and up to the breaking point? Is it possible that you are (or have been) fishing on the wrong side of the thing, like, the boated joint? Or even off the bay? Why then are you so empty? Am I even allowed to ask, my auntie? Okay. Go back to what you do, go and pray, but answer me this before you go astray. Is it possible that one could pray too much? Could it be that she's taking the easy way out of the rush by praying, my boss?

"Let us pray," is what they say, like, always. Have you got enough for yourselves and others, as it is, or as it's to be coming to you from those prayers of hers and his? Like that thing, there was, with those other fishers. "No." So, let fishers be fishers then, and let them go out fishing. As opposed to other things that they could have been doing, and dishing, or not doing anything, but wishing away, even. Could it be that Jesus loves fishers, even one such as Peter, more than a few other types of weaker folks, as is ours? No jokes. But I'm kind of leaning towards a "yes" here, of course, hand me one of your best beers. Yes, there, screw off the corks. Hmm, wow, this is good, "Gulp!" Thank you. The prayers are good; they have their place and time, as I understood it to be. But it just might be the time now for fishers to be fishers, like these. Be who you are, like who you're called to be. As for me? I will strive to be me, whatever that may turn me out to be. Till then, though, I'mma gonna go on fishing, or more like writing. Let the dead ones go on a-dying, even because of this. Or...

Pastors versus Altern Westview. Which of the two do you prefer?

Altern is here now. Altern is that guy who usually turns up at church once a year; he's always up to no good, my dear. Now, listen up, and you're more than likely to hear.

"Talk to me," said the pastor as he was delivering his usual, fiery message.

Altern: I'm talking, but you're not listening.

Pastor: You're not talking to me!

Altern: Yes, I am, but you can't hear me probably because you're screaming above everyone else, to try and scare me.

Pastor: I can't hear you.

Altern: Maybe if you weren't shouting that loudly, you would have heard me. Yes, they're screaming so loudly that no one else can get a word in. They are hearing so much from "God" that they cannot hear anyone else, or anything else, not even him. Seeing so much in the spirit that they can't seem to see anything in the real, as it is in real life. The real world that we live in is nice.

Elkan's story (uncensored). So, here's the story, the real story as it goes. Born in a farming village in the rural parts of the country, his own beloved tropical country. He's the second of eight living children to his mother (hi mammy). He was a bit on the frail side as a child. Not as ruff-and-tumbled as the rest of the siblings were and are. There were other siblings among them, too. Although his mother had eight, and you, the father's tally amounts to nearly a plate of... no, not of stew, but of twenty. It was the norm in those days in that neck of the woods for men to plant their seeds in any and every farrowed ground that's good, unempted. His sister was the only girl in the mix... her, at the time. The only girl amongst the mother's eight children and crying. Yes, there's a boy thrown in there too, one of a different father than you. But that is the beauty of the family quilt; the rural tropical farm-country kind of family quilt, as it is, right? Yes, right there for you and me, tonight. Elkhan was sent off to live with his grandmother very early on. But was sent back home later, to go off to schools of higher learning and greater, up or down. Might have been for some other reasons too, but... He was still much too young to fully understand those dynamics in the old lady's shoe and home, as seen coming from you. Family dynamics patted down to serve them, and guess who? Yes, Hugh, you know... Some things are never talked about in close-knit families like this, which theirs certainly was and still is.

"Right here is a good place for us to apologize to the said family, as well as close friends and acquaintances such as them, and you, not me, though, but some valued folks who I'm sure will be finding some things here to get mad at us for. But like it was said, in the hearing of some of you, even, under your head scarves. "Sometimes one has got to be cruel to be kind." There's no kinder thing to do than for one to reach out and try to save someone from falling. Or from dying sometimes, especially if and when they don't even know that they're dying. Which is the case now, and crying. Crying out for someone to chime in, seemingly."

It's time now, though, for the Elk to grow and go. Like, go back to his first love. In this case, it means going back to his family, up above, or down. The real family, not those other ones, nor the clowns. Those same types of families we just mentioned, for example, and those you love and want to... Not the adopted ones. Not the pimp who would have inserted himself into that hallowed place and trample his way into space, because he knows how people tend to think and feel about family, perhaps. Then such a person would venture into redirecting resources from the real to the fake. Yes, into the fake or adopted families for goodness' sake, my pops. Notice how they used certain words lifted straight out of the family playbook and from the family setting props? Yes, like: Bro. and Sis, for example, look, that one too, and this. Then insert them into the adopted family setting. Crafty indeed, isn't it mi bredrin? So, the Elk went back home to his parents' dome. He also went back to school to pay rent on loans and went on to do fairly well. At least in the standards of measurements for those times and places, and the rules to sell them as the case was, as you can tell. Like many others before him had done, though, it so happened that Elkhan was to eventually join the growing list of immigrants to go. Soon, he, too, was gone from far behind the farming row. So, for sure, as you all do know the score, wherever in the world they should happen to go, their church is going to have to pack up and follow. Elk was no different in this regard; he, too, was there, carrying it in on his head and shoulders, out of the country yard. Dragging along the whole mission, too, and the folders to get them across the barbs to you. But, as for you? "No more," he'd said, eventually. "No more will I cast my pearl at the feet of swine first, while the real family of mine suffers from lack and thirst, and grows to hate and name-calling me, as is now showing for all to see. How quickly the adopted ones have forgotten, though, and turned to doing just that? Go. He knew how it was going to go from way before because Elk had seen it before. You, too, will be turning around to give him evil eyes when he's praying, even when his prayers are supposed to be directed towards you, and for your blessings, as it says in... Your eyes won't be closed along with his, like he doesn't ask you to do, but you already know that you ought to. Or do you? I don't think so, boo. You will be watching him, though. Giving him the evil eyes, like so. Just like he did while you were there, praying for them and him. Telling them lies, sorry, I meant to say when you were praying for him, I, and the rest of the family size... way back when. Because they would much rather it if you'd bless them, all of them, the real family. In some real and tangible ways and terms to handle Leigh, when you could address them, and me. But you would have diverted the blessings to your earthly nestlings, the adopted, "fake families of his, and the 'Have's." Bypassing them, the real ones, leaving them out among the have-nots. Those whom you'd sworn were the reason why you were immigrating to go look for a better life for yourself, for them, and Gracelyn. Yeah, we saw it, we heard it too, we all did when you... We've all seen it before. How quickly some of us have forgotten, though? But as for you, yes, you, there! You wouldn't even know these things, would you, my dear? Because here this, and that is, if. Like, if you will now hear things. Will you? "Yay." "Okay." You were so busy there praying with your eyes closed, and your head down on the boards; hanging low, you know. Like, just the way they'd taught you to do it, long, long ago, so much so that you've been doing everything like that ever since. Not just when praying, but every other thing that you happen to do, or don't do, do, near the sinks. You do them all in the same way. Speaking of the prayer that you prayed. How well do you pray? How much do you believe in those prayers that you've been praying and would have prayed? How much do you believe that God hears you when you pray? Who is the God that you're praying to anyway? How able is she? Why is it that you only seem to be able to pray for those petty things, from me, and give us thanks for those same petty things, from her? If and when, like, whenever you perceive that something, be it a great one, or a small offering from the man, like, the dumb thing there in his hand, might have happened in your favor at all. You will pray again, and call, all day long, even, giving thanks to her. Even though (in reality) she might have had little or no part in the game season. Is this all that she can do for you, in the name of Steven? Such a shame. Or is that a reflection of your thinking capacity, to blame? If so, why then should I follow you to go, and your kind too? No, not when it's obvious that we're not in the same place as you. Nor are we going in the same direction, in this race, true? "True." But wait a minute, what is that thing I now see? The robots are coming, I'm A-warning you P, P.

So, while you were there praying with your eyes closed, several things were happening under your nose. Things that leave you just north of being dead, for the time being, mi bred, I'd supposed and said this to your toes, below your head. You're still there praying, though. If one can even call what you're doing "praying" for... Like, really? Things are still going on around you while you're praying, none of which is in your favor, but you don't see a problem, erring. Holy savior! "*You 'Don't never did see nuttn*" at all, I mean, you never could see anything at all, because you love guard. Your god is this, and your god is that. Your God is going to do that, and this, so relax and sit. There's no need for you to do anything but hiss and clap. Nothing other than to do nothing and p... like, keep pp-praying, and asking for mayhem, and money, all day in. From folks with the least of it, if anything, to pay him. Any at all to give away, giving it to you or them, okay? Or anyone else, I'd say. But what do you do, do? "Ask, for it shall be given," fast. Yay! Of course. Then you tell them that they, too, should not do anything, old or new. Nothing that might, in the remotest of senses, be able to get them out of the blight, and in a position where they can give a little bit more than he can. Like, like, ten cents is one such thing. Or even to have a little bit more, because to do so is sinful and worldlier than before, and not of God. But "Wait on the Lord," you say, to your followers and believers, that day. But you didn't tell them exactly what to wait for, to please her. Or what to do in preparation to receive it while they're there waiting on the knee slip. Nor what to look for while they wait to grease your hip four ma tick pocket. So that they may know what "it" is and get to know when it comes, like, to their gate near their homes. The thing that they're waiting for and praying for. They don't know what it is and won't know that it has come when it comes. Could it be that you don't know what to tell them, other than about waiting? While you're sitting there benefiting from the meager little that they have, on the plate thing, and hastening away? The thing they would have gotten from the other man and the date. From the government, not their dad, nor from other men who are glad, while they wait there and die slowly? But what the hell do I know, Leigh? Why do you hate yourself so much? Why do you hate your children so much that you won't even give them a chance to be born and grow up? Those who may have been born anyhow, despite you and your closed-up doors. Or even because of that, and some strange other happenings in your view, master Pat Madden, to the viewers. By you, even. Yet you say that you love them, but you still won't give them a chance to live and survive, let alone to thrive?

Elkhan did find religion quite early in his life, not in an organized form per se, but faith-based religion anyway. He had a hunger for learning from very early on, but with very little access to it, other than books. Whatever kind of book he could get his hands on, even from the crooks and the bad men, in those days, he would read. The most readily available book for him at the time was, of course, The Bible, said speed. So, bible study was to become his favorite pastime and liable to — "Oh! Take heed."

"Okay, I won't bother to say it that way, Ingrid." He didn't have a tutor or mentor. He would just read as much as he could know and would try to understand it all by himself as he went along the men's shores to grow. Probably why he's so messed up now, one might tend to say this while pushing at the wrong door. But, come on, now. He has managed to read the Bible from cover to cover several times over, by so doing. Not that that makes him out to be any sort of expert, nor a poser, Miss Sue, Hingh. A guru or know-it-all, whatsoever, no, not at all. But it puts him in a position where, whenever folks are going about talking sheets of nonsense. Look here, Paul, he can quickly pick it up and then some. Needless to say, he has had quite a bit of experience of that sort since that day, and so on. Elk was never much of a church-going type then, or, as some might have heard them say, "I was born and raised in the church." No, it wasn't like that for the Elk; he was too accursed, other than for the brief stint that he'd spent living with his grandmother, which was quite something else, or another, like, when and where he would have gone to church with her on a haphazard basis as a brother. He never managed to become a regular worshipper or church-going person. Not until he had grown up and on his own and worsened. There, too, lies another story as it is known by you. But...

Chapter eleven

Black Folks Sure Love Their Church, Boy.

One may well remember the rather large, towering edifices, those that usually take pride of place in most of our villages and townships' garages. "Society churches" were what they often referred to as, by the locals in those days. Probably still are, but... These are the usual culprits: Catholics, Baptists, Methodists, Presbyterians, and so on down to the Assyrians. But one did not have to look very hard and long to notice that these churches were (for the most part) empty in terms of membership, Bentley. On the other hand, though. Somewhere in a little corner of a village (any village) on a hilltop somewhere. Or under a green tree open up to the elements over there. A little revival mission could be the most happening thing you've ever seen going on anywhere. The black population is drawn to this sort in droves. Some are drawn in with purpose and vigor, others end up there accidentally on the meager. The women, especially, are always there, and everyone knows that wherever the women are, the men and children are sure to be following the car. One of those would have been there by accident. The men were usually there rather reluctantly when it came to the church thing, but very enthusiastically they were there joining up with those women folks and him. Yes, the children were the "accidents" that were to follow them. Music and dance were an integral part of the whole thing. The difference between the dance hall and the black revival Christian church was minimal. Only the most discerning eyes could spot those differences at times, ee, mi criminal. "Yes." I quickly figured out that black folks sure love music and dance, especially black women, and France. Francine is who I mean. Black women love music, and they sure love to dance too, just look at them over there in that tiny church, kicking off their shoes, and folding up their skirts to dance with you, see what I mean? Wherever in the world these folks would have happened to go, they carried their church along with them. Wrapped up nicely and tied up with strings and a bow, my friends. Imagine with me for a moment. Imagine a black church without a band, like drums, electric guitars, keyboards, organs, and microphones. Imagine a black Christian Church with only a pee on no... I mean, piano or organ and voices singing to someone. Well, you don't have to imagine it. Go on, push open the door to one of the established churches that we spoke about earlier on, in... you don't even have to sit. Just take a peek inside. What do you see? Oops, there it is. Speaking of organized religion, why is it called organized? As opposed to what, may I ask? Disorganized perhaps? It sure seems like it to me.

Liberty Hall, they say, which means anyone and everyone can walk into these black churches and do whatever the hell it is she feels like doing to go and play or spin. Any and everything she feels like saying and doing, on any given day, too, is a shoo-in. Tell me that's not it. Tell me that's not how it's always been, or go and sit. Come with me to the black church on the corner again, any corner. Wait there for a minute or two, my friend, before you're a goner, you'll see the difference. But what is the driving force behind this, what makes them function, or more like dysfunction, Al? Hiss. What makes us act the way we do and believe as we do? Say the nonsensical things we sometimes say, and do them that way? Thinking that we're doing okay when everyone but us knows that we are not... Wait a minute, scratch the word "thinking" from that, because we *don't never do that*, ever. By the way, those other churches, established types such as these, those we spoke about earlier on the hinges. Remember this, they were bursting at the seams, too, at some point in time. "True." But as for those people, like you, where are they now? I wonder. It's just something to put in the mixing tin and to ponder whenever you get started at doing the thinking thing. But please. Don't slander him.

"Oops! Oh-oh." Hey, you, did you hear that? That's her right there, your god. That's her there, saying those very words that you don't want to hear your physician, this man, or any other type of surgeon say. At least, not while you or your loved ones are lying there on the operating table to pray. But your god is now uttering those very words, in the hearing of nerds, even. Because she never did see this one coming towards her this evening. She must be pissed off, too, and boy, is she going to be mad after you're done reading this? Yes, she must be as mad as Hellshire Beach now, Sis. She wasn't angry yesterday, though, you haven't read this yet somehow, and all the way through, so how... how could she have known that she would get upset at me and you, for whatever there may be?

Have you ever taken a moment to try to figure out the behavior of some of those folks on the home end? Those folks who're out there trying to get you and me to believe in, and follow them and what they believe in, like the dome men, to save yours? Have you ever asked yourself, just what heaven will be like? The same heaven that they are busily trying to get you to, on a Sunday night. What will it be like if they are to get there too, as is, and if they don't change? Hey-hey! What a Prekkeh!

Sit down, servant, just sit down right here, in Liberty Hall. Picture this. She's elated, she has arrived, she's at the place of choice. It's a place of her chief joy, and she just can't contain herself, oh boy! She's dancing and singing along to the music; those pulsating rhythmic melodies, not you, Fitz. But the melody of her favorite songs and the melancholy. The chorus was to be heard ringing out over the cries and shouts; sit down, servant. You know, *mi kyaan siddung*. Sit down, servant. *Mi k'yaan Siddung. Sit down* — "*Suh wah fei mec yu fei kyaan siddung?*" Asked "the voice" of her neighbor, who'd happened to be sitting two seats down from her, and the Savior. And who (as it turned out) was her very own dear old grandmother; she who had arrived there long ago, yes, her. No less. Oh, sorry, folks. For those of you, "Other folks," the refined and proper ones who are still amongst us and still riding on the spokes. Here's the proper translation for you, of some of those words, if you're not yet up to speed on the lingo, of course. "So, what is to prevent you from being able to sit down?" Well... continued the neighbor, "*I'mma gon tell you what it is, Missy.*" I will tell you what it is that is preventing you from being able to sit down, quietly, and behave yourself beside me. "You're too darn unruly," she said. I think she was spot on right on that call, and the hot cornbread.

That's not all, though; to make things even worse, that girl is delusional. So, you thought you were going there, eh? "Right." Even if anyone could and does go there, you most certainly won't, you won't be going. How am I to be so very sure, and swearing? I'll tell you, my dear, in... You were told to sit down, "Sit down, servant," you were told this several times over. Sit down in the chiefest of places. No, not on the sofa but, in heaven's high-end graces, no less like a bunch of... The place you've always longed to be, and by whom? Who was it that had told you to sit down? Let's say that it was St Peter, perhaps, yeah! It was probably him, that chap, and you're going to disobey such a command from such an authoritative figure as that man, St Peter, in heaven, really now? Come on. But the real problem here is this: You, as well as the rest of the over-churched bunch of his (the crew), have been doing this for so very long (your entire life, probably). So long you have been doing it that you've come to think of it as normal. You think that this is the way things are done, and formal. Everywhere, all the time, and by everyone. You've been doing it in your churches there, too. One may recall you there, while the choir was singing another of such songs, crisp and clear. (You sure do love those types, boy). *Siddung, you know mi kyaan siddung, siddung, you nuoah, mi kyaan siddung. Siddung yu nuoah mi kyaan siddung. Mi gat Jeezas in mi swoul anh mi kyaan siddung. But really though, wawh fei mec yu fei k'yaan siddung?* Really? Could it be that it's because you're way too unruly? Usually, that is the first and easiest thing for one to do after a long journey: sit down. This begs a whole legion of other questions, just as many answers are waiting to come too, from home. Where are you going anyway? Where do you think that you're going with such attitudes and behavioral patterns in your play? So, as the saying goes, children learn what they live and live what they learn. You have learned some things well, no doubt, Lavern. Things like how to be disobedient, unruly, wayward, selfish, and the likes of flying birds, conchs, and shellfish.

"Let Jesus fix it for you," so they say. Or, Jesus will fix it (and go away), probably that, but. Are those promises right? Really now! What kingdom is there, anywhere, where the Kings do all the work, always, while their kingdom's subjects live in perpetual paradise? Am I even allowed to ask, though, and remain just as nice? Say what you want, believe what you want, for as long as you want. You're allowed that much like we all are, Aunt. We're in the business of belief anyway, remember? Blessed are we, in a slave town, maybe, same as how things are, in a blind man's country; can't see. Where one-eyed man is king, well, I'd suppose this thing.

I'm not your enemy, no. I'm not here trying to tear you down, contrary to what you might be thinking now, on the frown, yeah! But you might wake up one day to realize that I'm the best friend that you've ever had. Or the next best one, since you, me, and all of us, do have another guy; that one right over there, blue eyes. Some of us do know and understand that he is, in fact, a friendly guy, really. And me? What am I here for? A good question to answer outside the bar (or in), don't you think? I'm just here to point out some things that we, all of us as a people, might need to know and see. Things that were revealed to me, from long ago, perhaps... Perhaps for this selfsame purpose and reason, on the swaps. I wouldn't want to leave it undone when I'm gone, you do understand that one, don't you?

Why are you so settled in, though? Why are we settling in? Why are we so comfortable at the bottom of the pole row and sinking? Did you even notice that there, right there at the bottom, is where we are? All of us, together there, counting stars, and cussing at those who are cursing her. Why are we still so attached and aligned with those other people? Those people who have used and abused us, and our names, too. To raise themselves to prominence, in plain view. They will not even bother to come around us anymore, not even so much as to carry on the pretense as before. Like, pretending that we, you and I, do matter to them, or in their grand scheme of things? Yet they hang on to power and to glory, too, continuing to walk over me and you, more or less like making us out to be their trampling shoe. But we don't... I mean, you don't see a problem. You carry on gleefully like little children. Yeah, children are we because that's the way (they say) to get you up the stairway to heaven. Okay! I see. This is where you so want to go most, so much so that nothing bothers you anymore. Not even those things that your forefathers would have fought and died for. They'd believed in you, your fore-parents did and do. Our fore-parents believed in you, and me too. However, we over here in our current actions at the content boarding and unloading station, sure have forgotten that one. Young ones, don't you dare, don't emulate us away from here. Don't emulate them either, your so-called elders and leaders, at least not without first carefully scrutinizing some things like the issues. The past, the present, and the direction in which they have been pointing us as a breather for centuries. Like, to heaven, where we continue to point you, for the future. Don't just accept these things (as is) and carry on suiting her, asses. Not without first taking some time to examine these, my kids, and other such things.

Nobody likes to be told that they're wrong, not me, not you, nor that other one, dark blue. Especially when they're supposed to be in the know, like, in a position of authority. So, you've got to inform yourselves, like, assess things well, and analyze the situation, on the shelves. Use a value-measuring tool for each of these questions and be decisive. While you're at it, get to know what they can and cannot do to you, or against you, that will hurt you or hold you back, and slow you down in your efforts, and on your path. Because your efforts might serve to show them up quickly and fast, it will be the same thing that's going to put you in the direct firing line of their wrath. Be therefore strong and of good courage, to fulfill your purposed cup of porridge. They may try to get back at you, doing things that may amaze you at the very least. Don't get angry, get insights instead, like these. Some of them don't know any better, but they didn't want you to know that mi bredda. They have come this far, getting you and others to think and believe that they know. That notion has afforded them certain privileges over you; they're not going to give up those privileges without a fight. Right? "Right."

In the immediate environment and the grand schemes of their kind of things, they're likely to find great support in their fight against you towards a win. The majority of people will seem to be in their corner, to begin with. Don't let that distract you and spin the bandwidth. The majority of the world doesn't know a thing that is worth knowing anyway, that's why the majority of the world is in a quagmire today. But there's a small minority who do know, and what they know tends to govern the entire world. Hence, governing the rest of us in defense, including you, me, and the girls, on the bus, Ted, and the broken fence. Strive to be in that minority, if at all you can, at least in the other minority, who knows that one. Those who know that, although we are not in the top minority yet, we know that it's a better place to be than this. I do know that much. I also know that that's a far better place for us to be than this, for us. I will strive to be there. I'm doing this for the children, all of you, my children. Because that's who you are, mine, even though you may not know or recognize it now, like, at this time, but you are. Every last one of you is. For you, I will take whatever they throw at me from the car. They're throwing stuff out the window already as it is, but you're worth it, so fight on with me, brave soldiers. I sure will.

Why are you here anyway, in these parts of the world, to play? Why not in the other parts that look a lot more like you, like potters' clay, over where you and other people like you come from and rightfully belong? So, why here, and not there? Could it be that it's because they were here before you? Or there, whichever group you may point the finger at from here? What if you did point it at your elders? You will then need to ask, "Why did they (your elders) why did they come here?" What was it that drove, or drew them? What did they propose to do when they got here to stew them? Are they pursuing those objectives, to "Slew" them? Are they settled? Are they too settled to be moved? What causes them to become so "settled"? What's the danger in following their leads in that regard, if there is a danger? Or, if it is that uncle and his mixed-up, mixed-up family over there, or here, over here. Or anywhere else for that matter, my dear. If you did point the finger at your uncle, wouldn't it still be fair to say that it's because they were there? Wasn't it because they were there at some point that we are here? Uncle and his mixed-up family are and have been everywhere, though. So, whichever group you might happen to point the finger at to show, you might be found pointing straight into the face of your uncle, the great... "Oh." The one named Sammy or some other such thing to do, and crumple, and quake. His faraway cousin, too, that other one there across from you, on the high gate. Is there another way, though? If you choose to take the other way, will it be easy? Is "easy" the objective, like, the only objective? Did anyone else do it before you? Was it easy for them? Can you learn anything from them? If yes, what is it, and how will you then use what you've learned towards it, like, for a better tomorrow? Just asking, Kern small pit, no, you don't have to borrow... It's a faith thing, isn't it, Katelyn? I, therefore, am not going to be enabling you if I don't believe that where you're going is right and good for me, nor for the masses in the long run, and in classes before we P, and I sure don't. Why then should I follow you out? No, I won't.

Take a chance on your children; that's better by far, especially for your sons. Fathers, more so, I'm talking to you, not har... oh, take a chance on them. Teach them, show them, and believe enough in them to make a change. If there's a God somewhere, and if there is something that she wants you to know about this, too, she would probably have written it down in a book somewhere, just for you. A book named something like the holy bible. Or something like that thing to do, it's there beside you. If there's a god, she would probably want you (as a man) to first get to live a little and learn a lot. Like, learn some things about life and living, all about fat. Then she would probably want you to go out and share what you have learned when you're older and retired and giving, and therefore, you would have had much more time and knowledge on your hands with sleeve in. She might prefer it if you then go out and teach those young ones how to live proper and wholesome lives. How to love and treat their spouse right. For said spouses to learn how to work with and support each other. Like, how not to work or fight against one another, but work for the betterment of the home, the family, the community, the country, and its people. Working for the greater good of all who are in the vehicle, that's who. Be sure to teach them how to bring the treasures home and into the storehouses. Family treasures, that is, taken into the family storehouse, and such. Not to be fighting against each other so much, tearing down the family and carrying off the resources across the border to go and place them in the other man's storehouse, on the other man's table for his girl to go boast. The same one who had taken your father out of your home in the rooming house, and that too? It was because he was made able to go on.

"But, but, by whom?"

"Mi nuh knuoh. I don't know, man."

"But then again, since there's not the one, there isn't the other. Right?"

...

Why are you putting on this program tonight? This "no good" program? Who said it's no good, you'd asked? You just did. You did so when you'd said, "This is not going to be like all the others." When you said that, you were saying that the others were not good, just like you'd said the year before, and the one before that, too. All of them are now on top of you. Just in case you want more proof that this one right here is not good, wait until eleven months to a year from today, when you will be saying the very same thing, as has always been the saying. There, right there, is your answer about this one, my dear, ring. It's no darn good, you hear. But you're carrying on with it (as is) anyway. Because that's the thing to do at present, and it's for the causes; to prey... That's what everybody is here to do today, just like it has become the norm at this time every year, for no other purpose or reason. It's not because it's good, nor is it expected to be good and pleasing. That's not the reason why. It's not why they're here this evening, nor am I, no. You know it, and they know it too, that's why I'm leaving. But you didn't think about that, did you? Did you ever bother to think about anything to do, do, whatsoever? No, don't bother to answer that and be clever; we wouldn't want to make a liar out of you either, along with what we already know to be true about you, and all of the others like you.

Chapter twelve

L ittle is Much More.

"Little is much," they are quick to say, when God is in it, yay. They sure like to sing the song by that very name, too, and spin it away. Of course, little is much with God, as you see it. But then again, you can only seem to see and be able to fathom the little part of the mix, more so than the "much" part of it, because that's what is familiar to you, and for the cause of profits, perhaps. You know, the little part? It's familiar to you and your kind, too, no? Like, the $100, with 10% Tithes included, I suppose. That's going to be a lot of "much," as opposed to the $1m that was just turned down by the promising star talent of a sister, on your nose. The one whom you have made to believe was of the devil. No good can come of it whatsoever, Mister Huxtable.

Meanwhile, that same sister and her entire family languish in perpetual poverty and want. But you weren't able to see, or do a thing about that, or such a circumstance, such a pity, who does those sorts of things to me? Who suspends a brother or a sister from volunteer service in a church? Almost perpetually, he was there volunteering, and for what you'd asked? Why was he suspended? For committing the cardinal sin of writing a book, or books, just like other men did, and cooks. He then offered you such things for sale on the open market, to those with their hands in their pocket, hoping to make some extra money off it, at least. Money that could serve to better the prospects of not just that individual brother or sister. But it could also have inspired other brothers and sisters looking on, Mister, that they too could become another copycat, and do something with their lives like that. Just like the rest of them in the pack, other than continuing to do more nothing, just sitting around in the rings, doing yet more "nothing," other than waiting on the lord for her to come through and bless them, by multiplying their bundle of nothing, to make something of it. Just as things work in mathematics. No, not it, can't do that, nor this, which leaves one to wonder about it and to ask. Is there any relationship between your faith and your state, in the many and varied forms of the word and the dates? Like, your state of affairs, your state of being? State of mind of the economy? Nationhood or statehood. Like, your state and place in the grand scheme of things that's good, in the world, even? Could one of those things have something to do with the other? Am I even allowed to ask these things, my brother?

What about those pastors, too? Does one thing have any effect on the other for you? Does that very privileged position that she occupies, like, the gifts she receives to go in and "eyes," be it periodically or constantly... Does that have any effect on the types of decisions that she makes concerning the rest of the body, you, and me? Just asking, you see.

Like, if a man has two sons, and that man should have said to his friends in a conversation: they're of age now, they can't stay in my house any longer. Let them go out and fend for themselves, as I had to do when I was their age and younger. "Well," said he, rather abruptly. Son number one can stay if he likes, he can stay if he wants to, but number two has got to go. "He is a man now, no?" Don't forget that son number one, by that same logic, would have been more "man" than son number two. He's older than him, and you? But no, it's not like that. "He's 'Mannazzable,'" said the father, and grumbled. In other words, he is "good-mannered, respectful, and humble," continued the father. What would likely be the real story here, though, why one and not the other? Let's try to see if we can figure this out together. Could it be that son number one is more obedient to the father's will? More likely to be led and manipulated by others, still, including the father? While the other (son number two) will probably be more prone to be found making his own decisions, going his own way, and doing his own thing in derision. To his father's chagrin, even? If this is the case, which of the two do you think will be more likely to make something of himself and his life, in the real scheme of things, in your face? In the real world, too, with his wives, and become successful at doing it? I'm just asking this. But...

"Follow your dreams," they say. But whose dreams are they referring to anyway? Want to find out? Then, go on out and try your hand at doing something. Dream about doing something, and then go, follow through on it. Then go on further out on a limb and do it. Do something you feel you can do, like writing a book, for instance, and do it well. Just like him and you, then go and sell. You'll see. You'll surely see whose dreams they want you to follow. "Me?"

"No, mi bred."

What is destiny? Can it be changed? Why then? After God, your god would have said, "Kill them all," and they went out in search of them, to do just that to them; kill them, all of them. But after they came with trickery and would have trapped the people, his very own beloved people, mi pickney, you even. They'd trapped you into sparing them, too, no? No. Well, if you say so, Dell, I'll go. After those things, though, like, after they were to find out later what had happened, why couldn't they go back and fix it, often? You know the story, don't you? Go, and read it, go read Joshua chapter 9, there's a hint for you there, on those lines. Their very own god (it would seem) would not allow them to undo that mess. Then those same people were to become a snare to the people... well, I guess. God's very own people, and without rest, from then on, and even until now, well maybe, but they could not and cannot seem to be able to do anything to change that situation fact. They were not allowed. Not even via the same method the tricksters had used to make them bow to the noose, and borrowed from them that day. Destiny, or what? Whose destiny was that? What was the original intent? Which of the two scenarios was predestined for them? Which of them was destined to be so from the start, by the great god of art, at its inception? Or from when those commands were first given to you on the fork, to start and digest them? Am I allowed to Nyam... I mean, ask. Am I allowed to ask? Like, really?

My dad and mom wouldn't have had a problem with it, like, with me doing just that... sit, sit. Yes, that's it. That which you said I did, that had invoked your fury. How did you become so important to me and my life, in the real scheme of things? Like, with the wife, and in your mind?

My dad is gone, too soon, I'd say, went before I could even get to pay him back with the rod, you know, like, the same way he'd laid it across my back that day, long ago, "Oh, my dad." Hmm. But even before he up and went, I'd forgiven and loved him with such reverence. And Mom? She thinks the world of me, much more than she ought to be, and the evidence of my indigence is piling up high for her to see. Yet, my mamma loves me, and would not have found any reason to react and treat me as you have treated me this very day. And for what, because of writing a book, away?

Why should you test the spirits and the gods? If everybody were to say, "I'm right," and the other person or the other group is wrong. Or, even if they should say, mine is the right way. It would seem to me to imply that all of the others are wrong ways, wouldn't it? Wouldn't it be far more likely that all of those "ways?" Including but not limited to, yours and mine, and those in the doorways, even? Wouldn't it be more likely that all these ways are indeed wrong than for all of them to be right? If that is true, isn't it incumbent upon every person to examine closely and carefully what they believe in, before heading in to do it, and sin? What if, after those examinations, one realizes that what one believed to be right for all this time was, in fact, wrong? Should such a person continue in the wrong, just because she has been doing it that way for so long, like, all her life? Or should that person then contemplate an about-turn, on that very night? Didn't the lord (in the Bible itself) ask the people to examine, reason out, and consider things? To bring forth their strong reasons, and such the likes? (Isaiah 41:21). Wasn't that entreat designed to get them to change from one way to another? Change from how they were going, and start going another way down the line, to go in another direction, and go and find? Like, ways to start doing things differently? If so. Why then are these people so afraid of change? Why such a great emphasis on how things used to be for them? This would seem to imply that some changes have already taken place as it is, and those changes were not so much for the good of seeing the pigs. Or maybe... Perhaps it was not to their liking, more or less like the Viking. If that is also true, isn't a change back to where we once were, or where we ought to be? Wouldn't that be a logical "next step" for me? Wouldn't that amount to some form of change to get them the vex texts to read? Such irony, though. The opposite should have been so, like, true for you and folks like you; for people who are in the business of converting sinners into becoming saints, like, brand new. But what do I know? Nothing. That's why I go a-searching, seeking out, cursing sometimes, and examining things. Peradventure, I might learn and discover a thing or two, or even three. Discover some worthwhile stuff for me. Am I even allowed to ask these things, even via texting, three?

Imagine a song, and then begin to sing along. Well, if you want. Or start asking some "what if" questions, like. What if there... What if there were no magic, just logic? No spirituality, or even deity, but rather, just wit and common sense, as in the Eighties? What if folks were to start taking a commonsense approach towards things, what might the outcome be like? Can we imagine, for a brief moment in the night, and think about these things?

I never did know much (not that I know now either), but I knew enough to have known that I'd found purpose, possibly my true purpose in life, when I'd stood up, acted up, and spoken up, then I saw the people's reaction to the shakeup. Priceless. There are some things about me you see, like I don't like the clinging, so I went ahead and damaged the stringing. While they're dancing to the songs you're singing, I will rise, and I'll take to the skies because these wings of mine were made to fly. And then again. They seem to think that it's their God-given right to beg, so they come to you and your door, saying: You know I don't come to you a lot asking, but I want to ask you now, to give? What kind of people do those kinds of things, to live? Maybe it's because the megachurches are doing it and seem to be doing alright at doing it. It means that everyone should be doing it, including you in it. But you're not them, you're not mega. You probably should have and could have been more than just a beggar. Or to become, if only you knew how to do it like them, mi bredda, son. But what if it means that you have to show concern for the few, the ones and twos you already have, before you're given the more you seek? Or more like, if you want to get the many you crave, first, do this. What if you need to learn how to care for the few you already have before you get to the many that you crave? People don't want to feel like they are there only as numbers to prop up and feed the beast, the one with an insatiable appetite, like this. Then, when they're in trouble or are found to be in need, in a situation that could have been easily averted with proper instructions to feed... Like, teaching, guidance, how-to instruction, oh please, forget that one. Those that they never did get from you, Batman. Probably because you didn't have it to give, and the god or religion you were peddling wasn't real, therefore, she didn't know it herself, nor did you, or any of the above, but now, chew. Do you think that you have done well? Do you think that you could have done better than you have? Now the chickens are coming home to roost (meat to the hogs). Are you willing to let her, then go ahead and bed her? Are you even thinking at all, or is that too much to ask of you? Who does those things anyway? What kind of people are they? I don't know what to say about them, they... And about how some of us happen to behave, or more like, misbehave.

We love to talk about blessings, what blessings? What blessing is this when the very best of us have to leave the place of our possession, to go a-messing with thieves? Out of our birthplaces, our birthright, too, to go into the other man's territories, and work off our shoes. In those very places, he would have appropriated to himself at the expense of those other people. Including, but not limited to, people who were the same as you and me. Then bring the very best of you and me to come into their place and build it up, for them, and you gladly go calling and calling it an opportunity and a blessing. Whatever else is there to show, and there's no guessing. While back at home, your home, and mine, our so-called leaders are there busily trying to get the very best of the rest of us, to follow the same route, there in line. With the hopes of getting your remittance money flowing back to them, behind. So that they may be able to continue in the pretense that they are really something; that they're relevant. Our so-called political leaders, sure are relevant, right? "Right." The day is coming, though, a day when they (we even). The rejected people and their children of the evening will be accepted when what they did is accepted. While the other side's works won't be, like dead pigs. Even so, here's my question to Y'oah, all of yoah. These very people, this very church, maybe, this very man, too, maybe. *Is the status quo the way to G'oah? I'd say, "Hell N'oah."*

Oh, wait, there's more. Do you know something that the other people of the world don't know? Are you now, or at any other time, better? Can you honestly say that you're living better than others? Have you been on par with them, at any time, living well, living as well as the other people of the world are, and swell? Then tell me, who taught you what you now know? The thing that you say or profess to know that others don't know. Who taught you those things? Did your ancestors before you know that very thing? How far back did they know it, and coming in? How well did it serve them then, like, while coming in, and forward on from then? If you could go back in time ten thousand years or more and have the power to direct the course of your ancestors to shore. Would you have chosen the same path over, as they did? Based on the answers to those questions and the quiz, let me now venture out and into the boat and nudge you at the task of asking another one of these. Just this once, please. Why are you so comfortable at the bottom of the pile? Why is it that, even though everyone else but you knows you're at the bottom, the tail, the hewer of wood, and drawers of water, you are, in detail? Oh yeah, I know, that includes me too, now go to...

You didn't have to remind me of that, boo. But why? Why do you go around thinking and acting like that, saying that you are the head? Do you know what the head looks like, though, Ned? My, oh my, just a few more of those silly little questions for the production line, Baby Generation, of foes.

Chapter thirteen

What Kind of People Do These Things?
That family, what is to become of them? If there is a family, having "let's say," six children born into it today, just for argument's sake. Among those children are two boys and four girls, all this being hypothetical, of course, right? And let's say that the eldest boy (for whatever reason) has no children. The younger boy, though, has two, all girls, too cute, leave them. Of the four girls, two have children; they each have one son. The remaining two do not have any children like these. At least none that are alive and able to please. They're now waking up to the sad realization that they're all gone past or are fast approaching the end of the natural childbearing age, and therefore, off the bus. What do you now think of this family? Where is it heading, especially the patriarch of that family, and for his name and family line to continue, through the fuss, and spreading? The buck sure stops here for him, I'd say; the doe may continue, hooray! But sure, not the buck, tough luck. But really now, what does the future of that family look like to you? Is this the way God had planned it to be true? Your gods, even? Do you and your beliefs, along with your mountain of arguments and forbidding the breeds, have any role in what has happened to them? Am I even allowed to ask these things, my dear friend?

Hey! You there; this is not for you; this is for us. You're soft, cultured, sophisticated, and all. This is for another set of eyes to cry out over you and bawl. They know what I'm talking about; they're feeling me. They want to spill me now, but they're my people, they're me. My people know a lot of things, and they know me well, too. They already know that I don't know squat, and you? They know that my God (our God) didn't tell me to write that bunch of scraps; they know that our God doesn't work like that. They're now about to find out that although they know everything about what is to be known and shown. Somehow, they didn't know that I was going to say these things out of my reluctant jawbones. Things that God never saw coming. Now she's about to find it so disappointing, and therefore, I'm going to get what's coming to me. Because, unlike the anointing, no sin goes without a beating, you see. We all know that she's going to be fuming and weeping. When you're finished reading, you will have managed to see what's stored up within me. Well, surprise, she never did see this one coming to your eyes. No, not at all, guys. In the meantime, though, go.

Go ahead and care for those old folks, as said, those lonely old folks who have got nobody to care for them, in their later years, in the beds. Yes, do it, even with forks or chopsticks, do the right thing, and care for them in there, like you have been doing all these years, as you really should. But while you're at it, be sure to continue by not doing the wrong thing, by trying to do the right thing. Study the current situation; ask yourself some questions, like some "what if" questions, even. What was it that had caused those old folks, with no one to help and care for them in their later years, to be in the corks? What was it that would have caused them to end up this way? Was it just the luck of the draw, the way things turned out for them, despite their many efforts at making it work out otherwise, or did the choices that they had made have something to do with it? Were those choices (in any way) influenced by the things they were taught, and would have learned in church? Things they were told all their lives that they should or shouldn't do, most likely by other people like you, in the fern skirt. Are you happy with what you're looking at now? Are you satisfied with how things have turned out for them, your loved ones, your old folks, and your friends? Your family, be it the real ones or the adopted ones, as it now happens to be? Have you changed anything since you came around, anything at all that could influence another type of outcome for me on the ground? Are you doing anything differently now than you did? Is it at all possible that it was those choices that your elders had made that had contributed to bringing about this current situation, in doubt, and fades? Is it possible that, if you don't change some things, you're likely to end up in the same place, in a tight lid can, in disgrace? Have you been thinking at all? Are you thinking now, as it is? So, what is it going to be? What is your tomorrow going to look like? Will you be happy when you come back from the grave tonight if you find things looking the same as this, in the light, for these? Is it likely to look any different than this if you continue doing the same thing? "Oh, please!" If yes, why hasn't it changed yet? Just a few things to think about, but am I even allowed to ask it out, Red dress?

...

Now a child is born, what's next? Picture this one, too: a baby, born to you, somewhere, and tucked away in a tiny room with a table and a chair. A lamp, probably for light, and a bed were thrown in there one night. A pokey feeding pole comes in daily through a hole, with enough food and drinks to sustain life within, body and soul. Now, picture twenty to twenty-five years later, and that child is still there, in that same tiny room, near the crater, has never seen a fork or a spoon, nor heard of a witch flying in on a broom. What do you think the child's perception of the world would be? Do I need to spell it out for you to see? Yes, nothing more than those things it grew up seeing, feeling, tasting, and hearing, as they were happening around it in that tiny room, and wasting. Wouldn't it be how such things are?

Picture this 2. Now, let's take this a little further for you. Picture on through and in towards her... It would have happened upon a particular day that this same "someone," for some (seemingly) unknown reason. Was to have popped open the door of that tiny room, and let a rush of sunlight in, on the gloom. What do you think might be the thing happening to him here? Or even her, my dear? Those eyes wouldn't be able to look and stare at it, as it occurs. Because of the murderous, blinding glare coming in from the sun out there, which for the very first time would have breached the line and hopped up in there. For no other purpose or reason than to assault the stranger's vision and view of the great big world, now brought nearby. Yes, I know, I'm being rather extreme, melodramatic, even, but it's not without a good reason to cry... Our children were not meant to be locked away from the world and everything in it. Parents were not supposed to lock children away from the world and everything in it. But then again, what do I know about this and other such things to win a hit, friends? Nothing. Our job as parents (I think) is to train and prepare them for the real world, then let them go out into it and conquer it, and the girl. Or at least try to do so. Don't go about hovering over them like a chopper, all day long it's improper, and nighttime, too, or after. Only allowing them to go to church and come back again from church to look at you, big monster. Then go to and come from; home and school, because you must send them, so dictates the boss men, yes, the real boss, and the books of rules were the cause. Then you send them to more "church" and back again because you want to save them. From whom, from what, may I ask, my friends...? What's that? Let's now take a closer look at that, shall we? Let's look at another way of doing these things for me, such as: what if we allow them to start discovering the world? Which is, in fact, theirs, yes, it's their world. Theirs for the taking, of course, and the girls? Well, maybe so, or it should have been so, no? Yes, why not let them start to discover it while they're still subject to your care and supervision as a habit, and still on the go? Then gradually ease them out, as they gradually ease themselves into it, their world. Or into whatever else "it" may turn out to be for your girl. Allow them to go out and conquer it, and maybe, come in again, to sit, just maybe. And make you proud, maybe, while you still live. Just maybe. Why would you even want to deprive yourself of such pleasures to see, and the baby in the crib to feed, of course, such joy for me? Not to mention, depriving them of their lives, and discovering the boys...? Let your children be children, don't abort their development, nor quell them. Stay the course with them, let them learn, and reap the benefits, of course, well, if there are any left of it, like, benefits. Let your children live out their childhood while they're still children. But be sure to ease them good and proper, towards becoming an adult, promptly and with reasoned results, my papa. Let them practice adult things on the road to adulthood before they are all Goners and become just another no-good. Let them make mistakes and all, and learn from those, even by way of the falls, under the loads. Developing into becoming fully rounded people, down the road, and in. Because, ultimately, that's who you want them to become at last, and to be, not big babies like me who are dependent on their parents, perpetually. Especially, men, this one's for you again; you shouldn't leave them all up to the women and their mothers only. Not to their whims or all to their fancy, like you're prone to be doing back home, and cranky. Because that's who you'd be teaching them to become, women and mothers, only. All of them, homey, all of the time, by practice and all. If for no other reason, and the rhymes to call. Don't break your children's wings (or their legs, for that matter) by babying them longer than you ought to; it's improper. Allow them to grow and mature, broken bones and all. Broken bones from the fall, yes. Or from all the real-life activities they may venture to try, I guess. Things that are worth trying. But not the types of broken bones you're prone to give them, on the towns, and by denying... Which is going to be, in their minds, only. Teach them to see things through, and how to honor a vow, an agreement too, until they cannot go any further in. Then, tell them how to seek the exit, and when it, (the exit) comes, how to know it and take it to town. Be diligent and decisive. "Give no sleep to thine eyes, nor slumber to thine eyelids until you've delivered yourself, as a Roe from the hunter," and such. Prov. 6: 3–5. So, go, seek the Lord for help, yes. But be sure to first get to know the Lord for yourself, yes, to that too, and be sure it's the right "Lord," as there are many in that pack of cards. Prove her, or him, before you trust her too deeply, with anything. Remember this, or you're gonna weep, Leigh. The fake gods won't come to you advertising that they're fake and new. You will only know her after she has done those things that only she can do, and make no mistake. Know those things that she alone could know, and remember dates. Read and know your thoughts, and are not dependent upon mere words spoken, your words as they were spoken, on the half-hearts.

"Open your mouth and shout it, yes," they say, and I was like, rolling my eyes this way, and asking why. "Why must I shout it out loudly? Is the Lord deaf?" That's not the Lord that you would want to trust with your life, even after death. Your resurrection, too, after you're done dead and buried anew, and your wife? What if she weren't hard of hearing and could discern a whisper or even read a thought? Close-lipped swearing, too, of some sort? Can you imagine her sitting there, though, with her finger pressed against her lips, shee-ing you, like so? "Mind you disturb the neighbor," she'd be whispering it through to you and saying it that way, afraid of her. Or worse, "Don't let the enemy hear you, because he can hear what you're saying when you pray and curse and will counterfeit a reply and send it your way in reverse, but, of course." God is not like that, right? "Right." She doesn't work like that, sight! She can do anything she wants to, just like we know that she can, and the plants shoot. But as for that? She sure can't do that one. This and one other thing she can't do, now hiss another time, and chew. She can't bless me, and it's all because of me, and you? She wants so much to bless me, but she can't, because I won't let her. And me? I won't let her because I'm here doing all these other things against the cross (walking perhaps), mi bredda. Things she wished so very much that I wouldn't do, better, so that she could really bless me down to the letter like she wanted to do. But I won't stop doing those things, and try as she may, she can't stop me from doing them that way. Therefore, she can't bless me as she would have liked to before. If only I could stop, and I was just about to ask her why, like, why then, is she God, and not me? But that, that would be blasphemous coming off me, they say, and that's not okay. Who are you to question God that way? You know she can't, I mean, won't answer those sorts of questions, right? "Right." And what's up with those church activities you're planning for me and the little pickney? Aren't you using them to fill up every little breathing space that the children were given by the other guy? Yes, that other guy, even, in your face. By doing this, he was showing you who is the boss. Even in this action, he's showing you who owns and controls you in total, not just a fraction. But you want to fill up all that spare time with activities, you say. Those coming to them from you, to prevent them from getting into the wrong kinds of company. "With whom?"

"Yay, them, they." Or go astray and get into trouble. What if you were doing them more harm than good, though? What if what they're likely to be learning out there from Woodrow, while on the go, even, stands a far better chance of getting them closer to becoming fully developed, fully rounded, grounded, mature people, and aware? More than what you have been doing to them all this time, over there? "Beware!" Just look behind and around you if you don't believe me. But then again, what you see when you look might depend on what you want to see in the book to deceive me, like Fishhook. The same goes for him, not just me, yes, I know. You didn't have to tell me that. Although... How dare you? How dare you question her? If she wanted you to question her, she would have told you so, like, she would have said, "Bring your strong arguments. Ask what you will. Come now boldly to the throne," and such, and she would have written it down somewhere, like, in a book or something, of sorts. It would mean exactly what it says, like, ask anything. Or, if you ask me anything, I will do it. John 14:13 to 14. But she doesn't want to be asked anything by the neatwheat, oh! The poor thing. So, don't you dare do it, don't invoke the anger of a loving God on your choke... eat, heat it first, you hear! She who wants only that you obey whatever is said in her name from here, and without questioning it, beware, because you don't want to invoke her wrath on yourself, eh. She is one-track-minded like that and stealthy. No one goes against her, nor against someone else's ideas of her. So, don't go against it, or question the established norms and customs of the prophets, elders' habits, and friendship. The pastors, leaders, and the rest of them, like the believers... knock knock. "Yes, who's it?"

"*Ah, me, man.*"

"Me who?" Anyway, let's go... away, because those are all her ways and doings, if we used to do it like that from way back when it began. Then, it was the Lord who'd started it like that and got us started at doing things like that, my friends. So, it must continue like that unamended. It must never change as friends did, ever. Because if you even so much as try to change? You would be changing from the Lord's way to go another way that is strange, and would not be good, can never be good. No matter what anyone else might say or do to suggest that there might be another way to go for food. Or a better way to get through the woods, so, you pray, for jobs, of course.

Because one doesn't have something one wants, like two more dumplings, and another corn, perhaps, that's why such a person would have asked for it, right, Aunt Darcus? "Right." If so, and if over the years, you were to have noticed that you sometimes get what you'd asked for, even in those prayers of thine, to her. You might have also noticed that you do not have much of some other insignificant things, like knowledge, for instance, good health, or wealth. Well, you can scratch that one off the belt; it's not that important. But, for sure, you don't have a country to call your own and other things like that. "Mi jawbone!"

"Like what, the boy who is overgrown, Boyd?"

"Yes."

"Oh! Right." Why haven't you been asking for those sorts of things then, especially whenever you're praying? Well, if you believe that the god to whom you pray is as able as you say. If you believe she hears and answers prayers that way, your prayers, even. Why wouldn't you be praying and asking for these types of things, amongst others? Could it be because you don't know what you should know, and ask of her? Like, what is really worthwhile having in this, or any other life, or world? Or what is worth praying and asking for, of your gods, even, like, our girl? Well, what if that's why I'm here this evening? What if I were sent here to tell you... No, to remind you of these things, and buy beer and soft drinks? Well, no more junk food or drinks, but to remind you, mostly this, since we are all familiar with these and other similar things. Like, all those things to be known and kissed, will you still listen to me, even when these sayings are hard for you to hear and see? Will you allow me to say it, anyway, and show you before you shoot me? Would you pass up on that option and not bother to spill and salute me, since I don't want to die and go away, not yet anyway? Will you even spare a brother, an errant brother? Will you spare me? Please, please, please. Can you hear me?

Chapter fourteen

Chetalee, She's My Kind of Girl.

Meanwhile, Chetalee is still working there at the Mansfells' for me. She's now into "the church thing" too. She's doing quite well for herself, one might say, while thanking me for the red pea soup, on a Friday. But she's still working there at this point in the recordings; she has been working there for a very long time. I beg your pardon; practically her entire working life, she has been working there and has learned an awful lot on the job, too. Unlike most of her peers and associates in the religious circles on the squares, just like you. She has been setting herself out on this fabulous mission to do some progressive things with what she'd learned. She's different like that, and I can't help but like her, in keeping with these facts, Kern. The entire community stands to benefit from what she's now doing. Many other countries, too, such as countries from whence all the folks who are, in some way, attached to the church and its now growing affiliates, are drawn and drawn out of. The whole race, I mean, the entire black race, stands to win in the end.

"And in space?"

"Perhaps, my friend."

Chetalee was upset and utterly disgruntled at the fact that she had to give back portions of her meager, weekly paycheck to the very people who had given it to her, for me, in the form of payments that day. "For services rendered and labor tendered," they'd said, and for what? For something that she didn't sign up for at the start. Just because they could, they did. They went right on into her paycheck and took it out, before she even got it, out of their house, and the hood. She had to ask some questions about this. "What is it about? What is it used for?" They were taking a small percentage of her pay as her contribution to the fund, News Star, they said, towards the annual fund. It was going towards the benefit of the foundation. "Yes?" Yes, they said this to answer her questions. She did ask and was told this. What foundation? She had to ask further and hissed. You did ask those questions too, little miss, and more, yeah, I heard you, even before... So, she went and googled up the foundation and read up on who they are and what they do. She was angry, mad as Hellshire Beach's waters, too. "Why am I here, paying into something that does not have anything to do with me? It sure as hail doesn't seem to benefit me." But she had to sleep, just like everybody else, every week. She has got to get her rest, you know, to be able to function properly at the address and act by herself like so. So, she went to bed that night and tried to sleep, but sleep would not come to her to... weep. In the place of the sleep that would not come, something else came. It was an idea in the form of a "what if" question. What if we, my people and I, were to start doing that sort of thing, too? What if we were to establish for ourselves a foundation to do so? A foundation whose goal would be to support suffering blacks and others, like our sisters and brothers. Those who need our help, wherever they may be in the world, or on plantations and shelves, taking care of other people's little boys and girls? Yes, to preserve and strengthen the quality of black lives, instead of the otherwise... Because they, too, mattered. Black engagement, too, in our cities, our countries. Our very own home countries, even, and in the world at large, to provide a black and/or national networking forum for business. Individuals from all industries and professions are in these. To exchange ideas, knowledge, and insights. While at the same time, working to enhance the development of strong black communities and community leaders, to secure and mobilize human and financial resources was the idea; to promote black values and exercise leadership in the service of our mission. To serve as an investment in our future, and then it happened. That was her epiphany moment, right there. She went out and made her pitch to some other like-minded folks. Folks, she found there amongst them, surprise-surprise, those types of people were always there amongst them and under your eyes, even in the church. Imagine that, one, guys, and the federation was born. An ultra-black federation it was.

An investment in the ultra-black federation was designed to be "An investment" in a stronger black community that functions, for me, and was to provide the best opportunity to make a significant, extensive, and long-term impact. It was designed to be an organization with the depth and breadth necessary to support the community and evaluate the community's changing landscape. To rise to the greatest challenges of the race and capitalize on our most exciting possibilities was what it states. Both as a people and as a race. This was to be done as an effort to repay our debt to our ancestors and as our promise to future generations, not against theirs. Turning despair from other people's fear into hope for suffering blacks everywhere, and then the word started getting around and out of there. Then, one after another, these sorts of organizations started popping up out of the ground on the borders, across the towns, cities, the country, and across the world. So, there began the rebirth of Marcus's dream, to reclaim Africa for the Africans and our Queens, and boy, is it ever-growing and going places? It sure is.

Note: some of these statements were adopted from other parties and hence are not mine originally. I lay no claim to such.

The super athletes joined up. Timothy and Chetalee are collaborating now, and they've also been teaming up on some grand projects of late. "Wow! That boy is the real deal." Who is Tim? you'd asked. He's the superstar basketball player who came in from among us; he's making a name for himself, not just on the courts and the chorus. But also in the community, in the diaspora, and in his country of origin. Yes, he's my kind of guy and blessed in those regions. Timothy was born on the islands and immigrated to the land of opportunity, from the wild ones, to the land of promise. He arrived there with his parents when he was just three. Did well for himself and made good use of the basketball scholarships he would have gotten along the way, from me, no? "No." Got himself drafted into the NBA at nineteen. Has been blowing everybody away on the route to becoming MVP too many times over and often. Much too much for some of us to be able to keep track of, while sober, and gluttonously eating my mother's fried plantains. Don't forget to remember that he has been raking in the big money too. But unlike how things were to be with his illustrious cousin Vince before him, the man who went on a tear to the top of his game several years earlier, and went about scoring... Then just as quickly plummeted to the bottom, and then further into oblivion, no. That's never going to be the end game story for Timothy, not that man, and me. He would have purposed in his heart from much earlier on to use what he's got for the betterment of his people and his mom. From way back and for as far-reaching an effect as he possibly can. As the records are now showing, that's exactly what he's doing, and wow!

Vince made the money, lots of it. But as it came, even so, it went from his pocket again. Nothing strange to most people at the time; that was the norm, just the way things went, off the arm: If you're making the money? Your image and lifestyle have to show and reflect it. Lots of young men were making lots of it and showing it off. Speaking of shows and showings. Many people were showing many things in that arena, including the league's owners and merchants (mariners). To the detriment of many a senior. So, since most of these young men didn't have anyone on the home front showing and telling them the right things. Like, how to know what's worth spending money on, and learning the writings. They would have gone out and spent it on what the other guy was telling them to spend it on, shout: such as girls, liquor, and cars. Lots of cars, lots of very expensive and fast cars. Cigars, expensive Cuban cigars, and such are the likes of those are... Life in the fast lane has a way of coming crashing down very fast again. Vince "the invincible" was to find this out very soon on the crosswalks, down the lane. He wasn't so invincible after all; one was to learn that soon, too. Vince was very young and very impressionable when he was drafted into the league. Got comfortable and started making the big bucks, if you believe. His once hard life suddenly became very easy indeed, on good luck and charms, if you please. He spared himself nothing. From bright and shiny fast cars, expensive wine, and champagne to high-priced shook sisters and "whorshipers," as you are. Why would any single person feel the need to have forty high-end luxury cars in one garage, along with another twenty classic cars and motorcycles to massage? It's beyond me, beyond most average, everyday people to see. Ask Vince "the invincible," though, he should be able to tell you why, now go. You might find him somewhere down by the water's edge these days, roasting something on an open fire, flickering the flames he'd raised. Or at night, it may be under the causeway bridge that you'll find him, out of the lights, and trying to get some shut-eye in. Well, maybe. That is, if he hasn't swallowed his pride yet and accepted the generous offer from his cousin, Tim. He probably has by now. I've heard something in the grapevine recently to that effect for him, and so on. Timothy would have offered to house and care for his beloved cousin and his idol, Vince, who had fallen from grace. He fell out of favor with the league and from the pinnacle of life, yes, became nothing more than a common street bum. But it wasn't always like that, and more "some." Some people can still remember the glory days; Timothy certainly can.

Vince was an only child to a single mother. He grew up in the streets, not in the same sense as most of the so-called street kids do, so to speak. Vince was in the street, alright, but at the end of the street at night, the cul-de-sac at the end of the small street where he lived with his mother. You could find him there most evenings, playing with something or another. Tossing hoops, be it with a bunch of other kids from around the neighborhood on the border, or just by himself in the nooks, he would have been there. As time went by, he became very good at his game; my, oh my. By the time he got to high school, Vince was "The man" and cool. Fast forward six years on, and Vince is now in the National League, climbing up in the ratings; he's "the man," and they love him. The contracts came, the money came, and Vince went. Bit by bit, Vince was gone, bitten by some bugs from the wild, from somewhere beyond the fenced farm, and would not be tamed. He was never the same, ever again.

How did Vince get to such a place as this? What were the motivating factors and causes? His mother did try to raise him right, as far as raising him right was to go in the scheme of things (her kind of things) and in her mind's eyes. She did not have it easy; they did not have it easy. So, when Vince went out into the great big world of "The World" and saw all of the wonderful things that he got to see, and the girls. He wanted it all for himself and his mother. Started very well in that regard, he would have bought her a house first thing after signing the first big contract, on the card, or... then another. But the devil's playing field and the basketball court were the same, as it turned out, Vince could not see it at the time, though. Not sure if he ever did see it at all on the go, or anything else worth seeing in this life to show, not even on the call-up end to go. Up until he was eventually rescued by his friend and cousin from the fall, his now just as famous a cousin as he used to be, Timothy. The devil we're talking about here is that one right up there in front of everyone's eyes to see and stare. Whenever you're sitting in the stands and watching the scoreboard out there, like me, you're looking squarely into the face of the devil to see. At least the one to which Vince and others like him were to fall, flat on the level, mi P. They'd gotten the hot-blooded youngster from out there in the backside of the desert somewhere. Brought him up and under the bright lights of the big city, four squares. "To play ball," they had said, and that's what the kid was good at, and boy, did he ever score those shots? Like there was no tomorrow. But right there, on the scoreboard, on every side of it. Up above and underneath it, too, as well as any and everywhere one could turn their head and look at you. There were sleek, flashing neon lights, calling your attention to something enticing and very intoxicating, a vice. Something was always showing up there for sale. So, with one hand, they were paying the young kids huge sums of money, "To play ball," they say, while laughing at the funny — "Okay! I hear what you say, but, but..."

But on the other hand, they were taking it all back from them, or with both hands, my friends, not just from the steamy, sweaty kid with his hands there on the ball, but also from every other kid and their first cousin's bib, back home in the hall. Wherever in the world "back home" would have happened to be, those other people were watching and getting to see, yes, seeing what was being shown, and they were forming opinions. "Developing tastes, lifestyle swag, and habits to chase — 'Oh my god!'"

"Yes, he was looking on and saw it too." Or she. Habits that were influenced by those said flashing neon lights, and more of their finer things for them to go in and bite. Since the youngsters in those times, youngsters like Vince, for the most part, didn't have a clue as to what in this life was really worth working for. Or working towards, like what was worth saving for and spending money on, in the long run, and for the real good of themselves and their families, for their people to overcome. These young kids went right along and swallowed the bait that was posted, quite strategically up there on the notice board, and were roasted. Even in the sweet spot of it, the sweet spot of the scoreboard, that is. Right there for all to see, and stare, as you'll all agree. Chiefly those young overpaid kids, right there with you and me. They, we, all of us, saw it for sure, and it was also designed to set a precedent towards the fall forward, for more. For others like him, like them, those over there behind the door, chatting with friends. Every young boy wanted to strive towards those same things, thinking that that is what life is all about, and nothing else. Strange things, so Vince went out and bought what they told him to buy with all that money. None of those things would have mattered to him two or three years earlier; that's so funny. But all of a sudden, they were all that he was about, up until it was all gone out of his mouth. It all went just as quickly as it came into his hands, to a mouse. Then he woke up to the realization that he was broke and penniless, all spent and used up, just winging it. Because some folk never learn anything about the new cup or what's given in it. Who's up next? The wisdom of the earth seems to know what matters, so they set out to get as much of it as possible for themselves on the platters.

Since we're here talking about money, let's use money here as an example of something worth having. Money may not be the ultimate thing that matters to him, but madam, it's a thing that most folks can relate to, and it does matter somewhat to every one of us. Surely, to me and you... No, don't cuss. So, the wise men of the earth will go out and find the most, or all kinds of nothing to sell to fools for their money and to toast. Then sell them again for as long as fools will buy the same foolishness and the sailboats, like merry-go-rounds. The very same thing, over and over again. Hopping off at the same place where he'd started to tour the town. Just because it's packaged differently, perhaps that one, yeah, perhaps it was that. But fools would have forgotten that they already have it, and the costs were burning them hot in the pocket, though it did not serve them one bit, nor did it pass. So, they go out and buy it again, and again, meanwhile, the wise is gone with the money, the whole pile, making himself richer, richer, and richer still, all the while. While the fool buries himself under a mountain of nothingness that he bought dearly with his hard-earned money, to spoil. Or worse, with money he didn't have for himself, in his purse. Like other people's money, of course, then stay there and waste, die, and rot under all of that pile of scraps. So, Vince's rise was meteoric, and so too was the fall from it. But some people were watching this as it was happening, and all. "Oh sheet!" Among them was his own dear cousin Tim in the hall, and him? Don't mess with Tim; that boy is trim and clean. Timothy had a purpose in his heart there and then that he was going to make something of himself, too. But he was going to be different from his cousin in a myriad of ways. Timothy would have walked almost the same road as his famous cousin before him. The road up, that is, not the one downhill. The debate is still on as to which of the two is greater. Statistics are now bending towards Vince on the tables and crater. But in the long run, those odds are still in Tim's favor, since he's not done. He's still very much in the game and clever; he's having fun, playing, and performing at peak levels. The same cannot be said for Vince; Vince is done with the league, and vice versa. Timothy was sitting in the front row seat (so to speak) to have been able to watch Vince's story as it unfolded. He didn't like what he was seeing, so I'm told, kid. At least, some parts of it. So, he'd purposed in his heart that he would be different when... "Not if, but when." "When I get there," he had said, I will do things differently. The "when" of which he spoke then is now. It's happening in front of our eyes, and wow!

Chapter fifteen

She Loves Me Now, and I Can Feel it.

So, you thought that it was because the other guy loved you, that one right there in front of your eyes. You thought it was because he loves you a lot, that's why he did all that, blue eyes? Yes. He loves you, right? That was why he'd afforded you a place here in his grand city, those other valuable things too, and the pretty? All those things he'd afforded you, like a job for example, not at all, Nitty Gritty. It was love that made it happen, alright, but not for you, as you had thought and written right or blue. It was love for himself and his children, to the ninety-ninth generation of them. Oh no, it wasn't for you, oh, but... He did get out, this man here, yes, him. He got out from behind the bottle of beer and took your little piece of ground, dead Sin Ting. That same piece of ground that you'd despised so much that you'd considered it a blessing when he'd taken it from you and run, with them. He took it right out from under you, and from under your hand, then went to work making it a great city, and grand. Used your labor and all your other fine resources in the process to save her, and all other things pretty and new. Fine for him, not you, you never knew. You'd considered it rubbish, so he took it, all of it. He took you, too, to go and make you feel comfortable in a pigeon coop type of structure, the one that he'd built in that said city for you, on the cluster. In the city that he'd built. No, not for himself, he lives elsewhere and in grandeur. But it was for you and others like you that he had built it up yonder and rented it. He rents it out to you. Or sell it at exorbitant prices, too, to make sure that every penny that he was forced to pay you by some other people, of his kind, not yours. People who wanted other types of power and glory, at your hands and your expense, sieve doors. Yes. That kind of power, too. The power that those "others" were to figure out very quickly that you were the very ones who were able to give it to them, mi pickney. This said power, that he seeks, and the glory too. He then went on to make laws that force his brother to pay you for the work that he squeezes out of you, and only because... He must now pay you, because of those laws, and the Pay-to-Drive through in your expensive cars. Laws that could have yet benefited you just as they had benefited him. If only you'd gone out and done the same as that, and every other self-respecting person had done, with them. But not you, you just wanted some, like, something new to go around and mess with the screw, on a job. 'Because you're big and strong like that,' got all of the muscle that it takes to get and keep one to have, yes, a job. To keep you fed, and that's all there is to life, in your head. Your life, not mine and theirs, anyway. He invented ways to take it all back. That same little pittance of money that he was forced to pay you, on the fact. He came up with ways to get it all back because you never did care about anything, and won't be made to. You never created or invented Nuttn, oh sorry, I meant to say, anything. You're quite satisfied with what that other man may give you back out of everything that he has stolen from you, and out of your back, packed mi pops, to go and spend on a fat... piece of food. So that, if and when the pressure gets turned on, and up a bit (nothing new), nothing they can't fix. So that it becomes a bit more difficult for you to bear it, and function through the slit, on the little morsel that that said man gives to you to fit. Or was made to give to you to eat, by his brother the prophet, who'd profited the most. There are always those other options that you've got on which to fall back, to get on your feet again and up. Like street protest for instance, and sacrificing up your three sons, and your daughters too, in the same streets, comb your hair and come, even. To make them do it, because, if they can do nothing else, they can still listen, hear, and breathe. Yes, those people over there can still breathe.

Because they still have life, they can and will breathe. Your sons and daughters, though, no, they won't, not anymore. You've already sacrificed them up, for your bellies' sake, and the old bore in the cup, on wants, too, and more, much more. Like, the more bend to fit that you... Sorry, I meant to say benefits. The more benefits that you're asking for, always. But those folks would have listened, they'd listened to you and done what they had to do, they gave you what you were asking for, fast. Some of it anyway, some of the time. Of course, they may, they may give you more handouts, and more food for your mouth too, as always.

Meanwhile, your lands, the lands of your forefathers, that they'd given you in the days of the former, lay waste, and that same "other man," as well as many other men, in this case, with the briefcase, in his hands. They're eying it and biding their time until you're done wasting away behind your expensive window blinds, even on crime. Or become so used up that they can just walk right on in, and all over you, and take it away from, guess who? Take away whatever is left of it, from under you. That which was once yours, and show you a bit of mercy, maybe, by taking you out of your misery quickly and painlessly. You know he has always been kind and caring like that to see. But...

If you were there walking on the diamond and didn't know it, someone like the high man who knows will be coming soon, and it'll be to take it out from under you, to store it, and for what? No, not that sort, but... He takes it out from under your feet if you are lucky and sweet. But what the heck do I know about this, though? Yeah, I heard you, squat, Bro. So, it's not because he necessarily loves you like that, but he sure loves his children, boy. You, on the other hand? Yes, you love yours too, in some other sort of messed-up kind of ways and plans, of things to do. So, there you go; dropping them off here, you drop them there, everywhere that there may be a place that you can drop them off, on her chair. That's what you do, and then go a-counting them, one, twenty-two, seventy-three, and those three sitting over there under the tree, yeah! They, too, belong to you, not me.

Meanwhile, your children, every last one of them, look at them. They're there trying to count on some things too; they're trying to count on everyone else, and everything else, but you. Because they know very well that they can never count on you. Your female folks, too, and the mother of your children, boy! Oh, how well she cooks the well-seasoned stew, for guess who? "No Joy." But what else does she do, other than screw the cap off the oil can and pour it over them while cooking the stew? She leaves hers, yes, her very own children, to go off cooking and caring for the other woman's pickney dem. For a paycheck from them, for the money that she then goes off and spends in shopping malls and market stalls, their shopping malls, even. Trying to buy pretty looks for herself, maybe, and for the children's help, sometimes, lately. Decking them out in pretty nothings and shine. Putting it on them, but never even stopping for a minute to think about the possibility of putting it in them. Or something else, perhaps, like something of value, or just something healthy. So, they end up just as shallow and worthless as the other one. You know, the one who's standing right there before you in the shopping line, or going off to the Showtime, sometimes, in the same shopping line, even.

"Don't overthink it," they say, and you willingly obey. But what if they're preparing you for something that is coming along, down the way? What if they're conditioning you to take leave of your senses (of thinking)? Well, okay, let's just say... What if they don't want you to think at all, just take and follow instructions coming from them and wink at their beck and call? Suit someone somewhere just fine, one might think. And you? You went along with it to your undoing, we think, and for trying to fit in. Fitting snugly into it. Whatever you do, don't ever think, it's a very bad thing, so don't do it, I'm warning you, oh. Now, spit.

Have you gotten a copy of the Manley book yet? What are you waiting for? Training Manley is a riveting, coming-of-age love story, Jamaican yardie-style. Get your copy now on Amazon, or wherever books are sold, you know the drill, just Google it up.

Note: the Manley book was the catalyst for this book, it was this book: Training Manley, "the Manley book," that would have gotten the folks all riled up and got the author benched from activities in the church, and now, here he is, along with the old man, telling you the rest of the story from his mouth, to his hurt. Go on, get the Manley book so that you may be better able to put it all in its proper context and perspective. Out.

...

Purpose and reason. There are purposes and reasons for everything under the heavens. No, this one didn't come from ole Sol, Solomon, and the bold; you're too craven. So, just turn around now and look at the bowl. Go, what was it, though? What was the purpose and reason for all that he had to go through last evening? Could it be that someone had to walk the road all the way through? Someone who would be faithful to the cause, too, then go tell what is there on the journey, to the falls, and all the rest of the way through, for folks like us, and you? Could it possibly be so? The Elk is going to tell you anyway, peradventure you will learn a thing or two, and obey, get wised up, and start living to go. Not just praying for jobs that they may or may not be giving. Robots are coming, remember? What if you'd dared to believe what God had said and had purposed in your heart to keep your vows and the pledges, mi bred? "Comes what may," like you so love to say, Sis? As you like to say so much when it applies to other insignificant things, like they, them, and this one over here, whom I'm pointing out. "Hiss, then send." At the same time, taking time out to study and learn the reasons and the rhymes. Like, what she'd said about how to free yourself from such invaders, like vows, pledges, and bandages, and yes, that too, from Ned and Van's daddies. How to keep your eyes and ears open for such a day as that, and this? And to focus on such a place. Like, a city of refuge, for example. How to know it when it comes, yes, your freedom. How to take hold of it, and never let go, nor ever again become trapped by them, nor get entangled in the same? You know, the same thing as before. To follow her lead through the door. To go out and learn the ways of her working hands, her waste, things, and a whole lot more on which to gaze, Singh, yes man. So, if you were really in tune with these things, you'd most likely have known that it was her and him. Yes, it was your gods who had shown up to answer your prayers; your many prayers that you had been praying for long hours, or those that were prayed for you by someone else, in the shower, or while taking a bath. Someone whom you'd asked to pray on your behalf, in those days. She had finally shown up, and it was to deliver you from that awful cup thing. The thing that you were going through. You would have been wise, like some other people were, someone, somewhere, with a name unlike theirs, but like that, let's say, David's to be on top of it. Or something else to hit the spot, like this, just for example, my sis. 1st Samuel 18:5. But. You, too, would have been wise and played your part and waited it out. Because you'd want to be blameless too, when the day of your deliverance fully comes on the plain legs through, and you ascend to the throne, or to the place where you rightfully belong. But you're not familiar with such things, and the pain. At least, not that type of pain, what a shame. The type of pain that is designed to deliver to you something, sometimes. Like, from something bad to something good, or something better than that. Much better than the other familiar pain from your brother and the past, Mr. Woods. Those are the types you love, crave, and gravitate towards; you hold on to those for all you're worth, which is not much anyway, almost dirt. But you don't even know that much, and who is to tell you anything? Sure, not us, not me, not when I'm the one, yes, that person who doesn't know squat from him, and her. Nor she, in the pot of hot fried dumplings, and chocolate tea, as it occurred. But of course, if I did know all that. How come... how did I end up in such a spot, like, in such a peculiar place as that?

Something unpleasant is coming though, it's on the way, one can almost hear the chitter-chattering, and all the things that they have to say, like. "Yes, *mi did knoah*," I know, well, surprise-surprise, I knew it too, that same thing. There are some other kinds of people around these parts, who know some things to do, yes. But other things than those, it's not just you who knows. He's one of them; it's not just you. Although the Elk is that kind of person, like, one who never did know Nuttn to begin with, (the purse string). The Elk did kinda know that much, too, and more. He even knew that you would have said that, even before you knew any of it, in fact. There's much more that he knows, too. The Elk also knows what you're going to be saying when what is worth knowing is made known to them, about him, even. But the hope is that you would have learned the lesson anyway. Because it's for you, yes, it's because of you that I do all the things I do, for you. Yes, I do them for you, yes, yes, I do do do do do do do do do do.

No, I don't hate you; you're still some of my best friends, too. But while cooler heads prevail, there are some things we will need to talk about and work through, even with the nail. Take what is yours and leave the rest; they belong to someone else, one must confess. I just had to pile it all in this little space for whoever would come and see and take a taste. Remember what the old man says? No, not the other old man this time, not the grand one, but this one right over here on the other hand. The old man had said that when a leaf falls into the water, it doesn't rot on that self-same day but after. So, stick this one out, I would say, and see where the road leads, mi pastor. Okay?

Chapter sixteen

D issecting Vows.

What's in a vow, what does it say, what does it mean? Questions are those that need some answers in between. Especially when it comes to the marriage vows (and the clean), what does it all mean? Some women seem to hear only one part of the vow, so it would seem. Marriage vows, yes, the ones coming in from him. But didn't he marry a drag queen? Why else would she be constantly doing him like that? Like, going about making decisions and then dragging him into the plot, all day? It's not okay, the poor guy works so hard to make her big and strong, but she acts as if he's constantly doing her wrong. The records, though, will no doubt show how things go. The records will show that she doesn't give a sheet to the cleaning lady of the week for the bed on which she sleeps. But a thousand pairs of shoes for her walking feet was the opportunity cost of things such as these: Eyesight, seen? "Seen." *Yeah man, meat fei the yardman sin ting*. How about healthcare and shiny white teeth, like theirs? Among other such unnecessary things, gears to eat and share every other sum thing, even.

"Yu dun married to him arreddy," they said to me. Or "*Ah yuh wife arreddy*." You all said it, yes, to the young sister, and the brother, or to "the Bredda" instead, ee. "Bless." "Meaning what, exactly?" I'd asked somebody. Well, don't tell me, I know the answer already. Among other things, in fact, and very pretty, it's showing up in every aspect of your life, mi pickney. Change, it would seem to them and me, is a stinky, dirty old word. In your world, nothing must ever change from the state in which you'd happened to find them when you got there, my girl. Or when those things (or people) came to you (no matter from where), they must never change, ever. *Puppa jeezas, tek da case yah from the Iddie Hat*, because... That's why grown men are living and dying in the house with their mothers. The very first question one is likely to hear asked of them, every time one happens to run into them by the border, is: Where's your mother? And vice versa, swapping the asker. Because nothing must ever change from how you'd found them when you came. So your children spend too much time at home with their parents. How likely, then, are these children to become good at spousing, paying the rent, and prospering in relationships? If they should try and fail at it, like they very well might, given the circumstances wrapped up in parchment, and closed up tight, in a fist. Is it okay to send them back the other way, like, to their first spouses, as some people and churches are advocating nowadays to do? You do know who those first spouses are, don't you? Yes, their parents, their mothers, mostly. As it's become apparent to some of them. We're ill-prepared, unaware people, thrust together in the vehicle, probably living under one roof and driving the car, unsteadily, but doing nothing in common as they are, and envying me. Everyone is doing their separate things, not knowing what the... the hopes, dreams, and aspirations of the other party are, and in such schemes, as seen by far. With them being so set in their ways, they will not change, for all the gold in the world, not for the blings. Just there, happened together, and staying under one roof won't share anything whatsoever. Each one is thinking, saying, and acting out their independence there. Nobody seemed to care.

"Who are you to be telling me what to do?" Each one blurts out at the other foo... So, quickly they both forgot, seemingly so, Charlotte. Now they need to ask some questions, but don't want to be reminded about them, like, about the "who's who," whenever they're there asking, who you are when driving along in the car, and asking each other, "Who are you...?" Cross-talking the vows each had taken from you, mere weeks ago. Because, you know, vows are just things one says and uses to get what one wants at any given time, and on any given day. Then move on and despise it when it doesn't suit us, okay? Yeah, but unload heavily on those who dared to try to violate it and cuss, one way or the other, whenever it suits us, and the brother. Because there's nothing to it, on a toss, and backflips, it's just a tool like any other in the toolkit. Used by the wives of... sorry, I meant to say, the wise. It's used by the wise of the earth to control and restrain others, like spies, of course, fools, their brothers, and mules. "Woo!" But it didn't start there, not at that altar, in a marriage ceremony, properly, not at all, sirs, it probably began in a church congregation long ago. It was the norm over there; you weren't allowed to do this, and you weren't allowed to do that. But you were allowed to do those things and get away with them fast, as it was the norm with everything else there, and on your... I mean, in their class.

"Liberty Hall," they say, "Feel free to do and say whatever you want here." Yes, it's a place where anyone and everyone can come in and do whatever everyone wants to do, on any given day, too. Every day, as a matter of fact, and all night long and through to the daylight, look at that. You were the chief of them all, always having something to say and altering the call. Even when you have nothing to say, nothing at all, which is almost always the case. But you went right on saying all of your many nothings anyway, who is going to stop you? Meanwhile, what you should have, and probably some that you could have said and done, were left very much unsaid and undone, to the detriment of many, and that one. Those who badly needed to hear the multitude of sayings from someone there, which never got said by all of you wonderful Sayers of wise and needful sayings, for them to hear. All the willing and ready hearers of all your many wise and wonderful sayings came away from there not hearing what needs to be heard, to be daring. To the detriment of many folks and the preaching of the word. They were included. But then again, perhaps we're putting way too many things on some of your plates to get eaten, wrongfully marking up your slate here, even. Here we are, foolishly thinking and believing that it was in you to be giving those devices as advice, Sis, and wanting you to do those things, and you didn't. When in fact, all along, you were nothing more than... Yes, that one was nothing more than a blabbering blabbermouth who was blabbering the wrong things all about. Like, someone who just wanted to be seen and heard about, for all the coffee in Brazil in the South. Man, they sure have a lot of coffee in that place. Yes, lots of it, in this case. Now, though, it's all up in your face, go drink it up in haste, just like you're itching away to go and do; join with those who are there, drinking it through, with butter on the hotcakes, no? "No."

"Well, I guess you..." As for us? We went right along catering to your fancy. Your overinflated ego, too, the nuances, and your taste. Because you're the talking talker in the place, Pastor, but we didn't know any better. But, who's to be blamed? My, oh my, what a shame. It's probably why you have all those young people sitting there, fast becoming old people in the chair, and not marrying. Or doing anything else worth doing with their health, care, lives, and besides... nothing but tarrying. Because he (the brother) already doesn't have a wife, that's such a pity. Just his mother and his siblings, such as his other brothers and sisters. And that? As you already know, the facts, too, must not be changed, ever. Don't overlook the sister, "Look at her there, mister, isn't she sweet?" "Yes, but, but..."

"Yes, I know, she's sitting on it there, waiting, too, just across from you, to, to..."

For those of you here from the other churches, those whose pastors are doing the right thing and avoiding the curses. Like those who are progressive and forward-thinking. This is not about you. It's not for you at all. Well, except as a mere reminder to use at your altar call, yes, maybe. Or as a nod, to say, well done. It could even be a little nudge to get you back on track if you were beginning to hip slip a bit toward the cops' stun gun. But if this hits you square in the face, and you're inclined to get mad and out of place, then go seeking new ways to get even with them, and trace. Remember what the old man says; don't get mad, mi bred. Do as the Elk had done, in truth, get insight instead. Best to be that one. If you find that, that's a hard thing to find, coming in? Consider yourself as one of the other churches and pastors preaching, those fabulous "others" who are humming and speaking, ever after. You'll be okay, no doubt, my daughter.

"So let's remind them what would have happened when they first hopped in." "Yes." This new guy came in from the island and decided to join them. That was when and where it all started for him, and it began to happen, to try to find his son. He came in just like the rest of them: broke, had less than a hundred dollars to his name, and smoked. Got married to someone from amongst them, for whatever reason it might have been, and was soon to discover that she had little or no concept of the art of living, fat... or thin. Of what it is that makes or gets things to happen. Things such as marriage and kids, or how to make them work. How they work, and what was good and conducive to making them work. Well, maybe that one, more than any, for the man. But then there was more, as it would seem to me through the cracks in the door, Sam. Nobody had bothered to teach her anything. Well, perhaps they did, but not the things that were good and conducive to making marriages and such things as life in general, to work, for her and him. She did seem to have learned a lot of other things, though, in the meantime, and on the go. She was surely going to use them, like, every chance she got (or didn't get). But on this particular day, in the going-down part of a sunny way. It was to come home to the brother that he was selling himself short, down to the knee socks even, and on the prayer cloth, by planning to go and sign another agreement with his spouse's name on it at that, to believe in. "Hell no," it was to go... What if, like, while he slept, his wife was mischief-making, yet? The very person who (if I'm to be certain) should have been his helpmate, and nice. His friend, too, and confidant, his virtue, is like a good wife. "A virtuous woman you are," and the one who weaves with her hands and sells it to buy the car. Clothed her household in scarlet. She considers the field and buys it, brings treasures home into her household to upsize it for them, instead of digging under the foundation of gold, and despises it while pulling the rug out from under her husband's feet. Her beloved, her strength, her god that he is, while he slept, even? What if she was busily making mischief for herself and her family all evening, while her husband slept, hard breathing and snoring? By going shopping for things she didn't need, didn't even want, the poor thing. You can bet on that one. They (definitely) could not afford it, but she was shopping anyway, with the cards, Sis. With other people's money, yes. Because she didn't have any at the address in the yard, as it was. Mortgaging the money they didn't have, (oh lord, what's this)? So, she borrowed it, or charged it to those cards and misfit, to further enrich the credit card companies, yes, to his credit card she went, and further into debt. Not her cards yet, though, because this one is already overspent, so she uses his. Without permission so to do, Sis. She never did seem to know how it or any other such thing works, no matter how much others who know and understand the corks might have tried to tell her, because... well, whatever. They were always telling her how those things work. But she just carried on to the beat of her drumming, tam, tam, tam, because she thinks these things are magic. Or blessings from the man, or something else wonderful, and not tragic. Oh, come along. No more guessing. They all come to her to bless her, not him, and the cost and price for her go away into thin air, and her husband always seemed to her to be able to make them do just that, disappear. Like, make them go away, and fast. Like magic from the glass, of course, and stay away from your rasp... at last, as it occurs. So, she does it all the more, yeah! Then came the day of reckoning, as it is today, well, probably, but...

...

"*A yuh wife Arreddy,*" so they said. Which seems to me to mean, you've already married her, mi bred. There's nothing you can do anymore, other than to stay, till your dying day, not before. That is where the emphasis lies, as far as they're concerned. That's where the matter ends, too. Unconcerned, there was not much coming from them to her to get her to take notice of some things she was doing. Because her work was already done (it would have seemed to Mister Ross and his sons) on the very day she married you and him, my son. So too were her worries, and she? She knows that she's got all the cheerleaders in her corner. Quite unlike how things are with her husband and you, who are now goners. She can do no wrong, in this neck of, come on, sing along with me now; la-la-la-la, la-la, land.

But as for her husband? Unlike how it was with others who were there and looking on, he had purposed in his heart to see it through. He was trying to prove his god against the rest of the scouts and you. To see if she's any different from all the other gods, not just a bag of mouth, Bagga boo, in the crew. Like, if she is a covenant keeper, or if she (by any chance) were like me, living on fees. Does she love covenant-keepers, like her and me? Would she be able to one day reward such types, in the eyes of the unbelievers, those who gripe at the naysayers, even while tossing away our resources on the wipes, for no good reason? So, he'd propose to bear it all by himself and press forward. Doing whatever it was that he needed to do, amid all the ridicule, too, let's go to Harvard. Will the real god show up now, or at any other time to deliver? Or is it the wrong gods that we've been worshipping, all along, on the river? Like, forever, and ever, amen, and the real one can do nothing about it, even if she tried, and was to be found fit? If so, why then should we bother? Why should anyone bother? Is such a god going to be able to take our bones out of the grave, where they are going to stay anyway? Right there in the grave is where they're going to stay, and in their grave clothes, too. This is where we are all going to lie when they are done burying me and you, okay? Well, I think, yay! But until that other day, the one of which they speak and pray. If there should ever come such a "way," in keeping with what you're hearing them say at funerals, or whenever your loved ones are dead and passed away, like the two generals. But this kind of talk, too, is not okay, it's not allowed, and I'm sure that somebody is going to be made to pay for this, too, and be proud, yes, for real.

They don't vote either. Ask them to go out and cast a vote on Election Day, and you'll see. One is likely to hear words such as these: I don't vote, I've never voted a day in my life. Or my favorite of them all, *"mi*

Ungle vote feh jeezas crice an him crucify." Okay, let's say it this way: I only poll a vote for Jesus Christ, and him, crucified. And I was like! That's probably why they're crucifying your sons and your daughters in the streets at night, or even in the glare of the sunlight, constantly. While you and your kind of people pray, march, and protest, because that's how to get things done for me, yes. In your mind, perhaps, and then some. But in the real world, the vote count goes a long way. Longer than your girl's long, beautiful legs across the doorway, even. But you don't know that and won't know because you never bothered to stop and consider the facts. Meanwhile, other people, like those who would have started coming in long after you, on the vehicle, ride. They've been making great strides; they've gone a long way past you. They're gone ahead (or two), leaving you covered with dust. Ask who? Yes, that's it, the dust of their passing, no, not that. Not "passing away from us," as you would have liked and wanted. But as they go and pass you by on the bus to rawtid. Even in your most treasured things of all, like storing them up in the kingdom hall, look up there on high. They have been building too, putting up great edifices. Woo, look! Monuments are going up, to the glory of their myriads of gods, and their marvelous works. While you are still there, like, worshipping in hovels and corner shop types of shacks, on the square, like a jerk... chicken, perhaps. Talking about winning people to Christ, bringing them back, what people are you talking about? What people do you hope to win like that? Oh, don't bother to answer me back on that either; we all know the answer, and it's meager.

Picture this. Look, head hanging low, as she sits in a chair. The sullen-faced judge in the high chair, there, looks... Across the way sit twelve other sullen-faced individuals, none of them even looks like him, or the little gal, but. Just like things are with my meager pal, they're, nonetheless, there. They're there to judge him and to decide on his fate. His mother prayed a lot to wipe his slate. She always does that, she prays, if nothing else, in those days. She was sitting in the courtroom, too, a crowded courtroom, yes, across from you. Having been there since the early morning, now it's the afternoon, and her stomach is calling. Her son was framed; she knew it. She knew very well that he didn't do it; he was born and brought up in a church. To take and put him away from her is surely going to hurt more than words could ever say. But she's here today, and she'll continue to pray. However, she doesn't like the looks of that awful judge and the jurors. They won't seem to budge against our words. Mom is still sitting there, but then it was to hit her in the square of... Those people over there are not with her. "From amongst your peers, they are taken." So they were heard saying in the answer to her hidden questions, and while she shakes, at them there, still shaking... yes, their hands, Sir. "Was... wasn't it...?" "No, not that, but... But none of them look like me anyway." Then came the big question of the day. The question is as to how, where, and why. How did it all come to this? My, oh my. Where, where did all these people come from? Oh sheet! She hissed her teeth: How did they come to be the ones sitting up there on the stand, and not me? Ah, ah, a wake-up call for you, Mom. It's time for you to take a closer look at some things and how they're done. It's time to learn how these things work on the home front, to help them in their work, to perform. Those people have names, you see, just the same as you and me. Yours could have been on the voters' lists, too, marked as having polled a vote, but as for you, nope, I know. You didn't know that much, nor the way out, did you? The place where they'd found those names? From the most recent municipal enumeration (voters') lists, amongst other such things as this. But you couldn't bother with it, you wouldn't be bothered, oh sheet, my brother, and then again. They were heard discussing and debating, too, on recent election platforms, and in our view. They were being asked questions, among them were these, to address them, or this one; questions as to how things should be done in a multicultural city. "But minorities," they said, "are not treated equally, they are not properly represented currently. Are you going to do a study on minority issues in the city and in the state?" (Or in the province, as it was, in this case)? "No, no, no." No was the conclusive answer, long ago, every last one of them; the politicians and friends standing there. They all were heard to have said "No." That was the answer, coming in sure and slow, in their responses to the asking person, on the ego. The people who mattered in any and everything concerning your life, and mine. The way you live and get things done all the time, in this business, I mean, in this place you now occupy, live, and call it home as it is. Every last one of them, with no exception, from friendly pigs, was quick to say no, and why should they go any other way, though? There'll be no benefits for them in trying to do anything for the likes of you and me, nor him, Mass Keith E Mingh. Not on any given day, because. We, the collective, "we," know the causes since all of the records did show that you? As such things go, don't "Never" go, and poll a vote, either. Not ever. *Mi vote feh Jeezas Crice only*, and him crucified. That's how they lied, every time. So, why should they bother with things like mine? Like the politicians and others. Why should they bother with people who can't be bothered? What's in it for them? Nothing. But other people will rally and make the politicians stand up and listen, take notice of them, and give them what they want, in exchange for their vote in the end. Not you, though, you didn't know. So, you sit there and wonder. How come they, the newcomers? How is it that they are doing so very well, but you, who have been here long before them, can't ever seem to be able to get a breakthrough to heaven, to the kingdom, even? Well, now you know why, I hope so. But do you? Nope... no.

Chapter seventeen

The Pardels Came in Among Them.

This is the "love" that I'm feeling. Hey, you there, fix your face, drop that frown, and put a smile in its place. You're taking things way too personally, Grace. It's true, this is not about you. It's about us, all of us. The man doesn't hate you, as you might have thought. Get that notion out of your head, boo, you're smart. Get it out of your mind, this is love at its finest that one may ever find. Yes, love for you, love for himself, love for me. Love for all of us as a family. Love for a people like these, even.

So, when next you happen to look around you and notice that your dear friends and acquaintances are gone, the best and most promising prospects of the year... no, don't, don't yawn. Those who were there from the inception of the mission and moved on. Yes, they're all gone, just as you were beginning to feel like you were getting somewhere with them, the program, and Mom. You were even on the brink of a major breakthrough at the time, come on. A breakthrough that included the sister and the brother, too, so you thought. But woo! They get up and leave, just like that. Yeah, just like thieves in the night's dark, "Almost simultaneously," I heard someone say to me. It wasn't a plot against you, no, nor was it a conspiracy to take you down in rank. It's just people at their fabulous best, doing what people do best in finding rest; making statements with their feet as walking friends, and with their walking shoes toeing the mountain range. Mobility, that's her right there, a great defender of peace, in the walking pair. Bringing a little piece of..., you know, among the brothering over there. The brother and the sister didn't just suddenly wake up and realize that they no longer loved their lives living there in that city. It probably wasn't even that great a job either, you know, the offer. "What a pity!" The offer they'd gotten coming out of the other faraway city, to them, wasn't an offer they couldn't refuse. No, not necessarily so, Ms. Hughes. The sister was the very person who'd sought the job in that faraway city, way ahead of the time of her leaving this city, and you, such a pity. Yes, leaving you and your circle, too, and all that you're doing over there, or not doing. From what you're trying to do there now, and spewing more hot air, of course. The sister made a statement with her feet, you know, yes, with mobility, to keep the peace. In so doing, she didn't create animosity or make enemies out of her loving friends. No, no enemy was made on that call or in the process of getting it to the end, like, making it to heaven. Nor did she create any bad blood amongst the people she dearly loved, you even. In doing it that way, she'd ensured that, every once in a while, she could still drop in on you, and on all the other friends of yours, too. She can still feel and share the love whenever she does it in style. The fellowship, too, will remain intact, no hard feelings from the hand-shaking gloves, not with you, now smile and stop... But sis? Sis had had her fill of the foolishness. Yes, the deadness, as it was, and still is. The deadness of the unenterprising enterprise that wasn't going anywhere at your address and before her very eyes. No, no surprise. At least, not any place that she'd planned on going, you know! Like, with you towards success, and other such achievements to show him what's next. So, sis is gone, and so too is Bro, and his mom. Others came in after them, and they're gone too. "Oh no!"

"Oh yes, it's true." They also went, as said. But you're still there, growing more, or not growing, other than for growing frustrated at not growing, not seeing the results you'd longed for, and slowing. At what you'd labored for. Yet you keep on keeping on, beating away at the rhythm of the same drums and hoping that the change will eventually come. No, my king, take it from this fool right here, watching, it won't, that change will not come. Not if you continue to do the same thing, in the same way, like a numbed... The change you seek will not come under those conditions. That breakthrough that you seek will not come, not under the rhythm of the same beating drums.

As for you, young ones, hats off to you, and the fun ones, to some fabulous others here too. Take a bow from guess who? Yes, me, because you've done well. You're doing well even now. I just wanted to say a big thank you to you. Wow! You've already begun to prove this old man wrong. You're reading this, which means you're reading, an instant improvement from where we, as a people, were this evening, from where we are coming, too. I hope to find you writing when I come back, true. Or, whenever I finally grow up and become a man out of this little brat that I am. Well, if I should ever, and don't let nobody... I mean, anybody. Don't let anybody stop you from writing. Once you get started, continue writing and reading, my star king. That's the right thing, trust me on this, they will. They will try to stop you, but don't ever let them. After you're done with reading this stack pile of scraps right here, don't stop there. Whatever you do, don't stop reading. Be sure to go over there and read some real writings of the real authors, the real philosophers too, and such the likes as her, no, not you. You already know that I don't know much. So I wouldn't even know who, or what... like, what to tell you to go out and read that might be worth reading, as a start. But you can start with books such as Pride and Prejudice, while you're at it, go learn how to kill a ...kingbird, sorry, I meant to say, "a Mockingbird, like this" To Kill a Mockingbird. You might even want to throw a Moby "Dick" in there somewhere, too. I'd heard some rather smart folks talking about those, so they must be good, as I'd supposed. I will try to read even one of those myself. Well, one day perhaps, like, when I'm grown up and get to pass my reading class, exams. But as for you, go ahead, read, read, read books, as said. That same book over there in the little nook, even, as you've never done. There are some treasures bound up beneath the pages of those books for the ages, even that book, on your gown. But don't tell anyone that I told you this, it's not safe, my sis, so. Don't let them know that you know these things, alright? Deal?

"Yes."

"Okay." Did you know, though, that those who will try don't even have to know how to do things? Once you've started trying? You'll be enabled and helped along in the lord's rings. You will be shown how it's done by those who happen to know how it is done, among other things, to add to the sum. Try it out and see. Listen to me, my people. Go to school and learn the rules, learn to read. Be sure to read this book, even, it's a good place to start this evening or go to church. Continue going to church, and praying, and prepare to die, only, and go away. Like, remain dead, and then die again. Then go off to heaven, to stay, amen. You know, you've been doing so for way too long, and nothing else, mi bredda man. When a man has done his best, let others do their piece and go to the show at "The Summerset in the Netherlands." Everyone's work will (in time) face the test, and— "And, and the wild beast, no?"

"Oh yes. Well, I think." But what do I know anyway? Nothing.

There once was a girl, a beautiful church girl. Oh, how much he loved her; he still does. He would have climbed the clouds and picked her a star. But she wouldn't let him inside the car, because it was the wrong thing to do with Har, I mean, her. They couldn't do that. She would have done some things, however, on the spot. They would have done some things together, other things like that. Things one might have thought she, I mean, "they," them and him, shouldn't have had any business doing. But she did those things to him; they did those things. But there was one thing that she wouldn't do, "No matter what." Because she couldn't do that, she wouldn't love him back, no. She couldn't do that. She couldn't love the brother back. At least not like that, no matter what, because God doesn't work like that. In all of her knowledge and the "knowing" of those and other such facts and things she'd learned in college, she did manage to learn that much from spins in cornmeal porridge. She knew all along that God didn't work like that. Then there was yet another girl, one whom I, even I, would have sought out and pursued. We did things too, like make a promise to be married to each other, and have me excused. No, not you. We had started the process to do so, but then, it all ended upon the introductions of some friends where they should not have been, at least not in the then-current schemes of such kind of things. But it all came to an end when it happened, and then, other things were to happen, which left one not guessing that this too was divine intervention, coming from who? Yes, him, coming to him in the end.

You didn't know this, though, I'm sure. Yeah! I heard you. You're so smug and secure in your self-satisfied heaven, are you not? "I knew it," I hear you say, "he got what he deserved, he got what was coming to him in reserve. It was coming all along," you'd said. You couldn't be more pleased. "I told him", another one among you had said, "Echem! Excuse me, please, that was a sneeze."

"*Mi knoah, mi did tell him though, mi bred,*" but he would not listen; now it is payback time. "*Nuh ramp wid god,*" said another one. "Caz, God nuh play, seet deh, mi did knuoah." Yes, look at it. So, what are you going to say tomorrow, may I ask? What will you say tomorrow when the table turns in my favor so you can pass? Like how you would have squeezed through this small space and passed me by. Well, perhaps? It most certainly will happen like that if it takes forever on a high hat. When the other God, the God whom you and those around you do not know or serve. What will you do after she comes to my aid and to preserve... what will you do then? Or when she shall come to show who it is that she has chosen, as a friend? The one in whom she is "well pleased." The one whose olive stick would have spouted, like these, would have grown and borne fruit for you? What are you going to say and do then, my youth? Will you be willing then, to put away the fake for real? Will change become a viable option for you and yours then, my friends, on the deal? Just asking. I'm allowed to ask him, am I not?

18 |

Chapter eighteen

The Invitations Came.

They talked of love and about having babies. Then they went out and did just that, no maybe's, and now... While your mammas are busily wiping said babies, assuming things, and calling him Massa, on top of the stinks, your mamma is not much in their eyes. But as for my children? "Who do they think they are, for coming up in here...? (As they were to hear). Or going up in their hallowed places on the thoroughfares, acting like they are, when everyone knows, they ain't even sheet?" That's the way they see it. So, my question to you is: what is the difference between that other man's child, whom you innately call "Massa," while wiping him away with your motherly love, of sorts? What's the difference between his and mine, my children? Children who you don't ever wipe, even though they're as clean as a whistle tonight, or till then. But you don't think that they are sheets, whether it be white, yellow, or pink, and neat. What's the difference between the two here? Could it be that it's the money, the thing that you love so much that you will do anything and everything just to get your hands on some of it, but never have any, to give anybody? Including, but not limited to, beguiling other people's children into bringing their gifts to you. Monetary gifts mostly, and laying it all down at your feet to slow sleep, in truth? Then, if and when you should find out that they really don't have it, like they'd been telling you all along, but you would not hear any of it. You turn to try and extort it out of their parents' pockets, with trickery too, and through the slippery fingers of those said children of his, who… When that also turned out to be an effort at futility, since the parent, too, didn't have much of it yet either, for your utility. Like you'd thought, because of what you would have seen, probably. You were more than ready and willing to toss our child under the bus, before going straight back to your whippy wiping job the following morning, and into the fuss? Could it be the money that would make you want to do those things to them, and us? Would we be right in thinking that this is also the very thing you never bothered to learn how to keep any of? Could it possibly be that? Could it be the money that that man and his kind pay you for doing the work, that type of work even, for him and his kind of… while they go out and get paid, all of it, the real pay, all the time? Then allow just that much to keep you coming back for more, yes, more of the next-to-nothing you have been getting before? Like, from the lord's storehouse, and the other stores, and glorying in it, same as before, calling it a blessing, and all other such things? While you and your children (and mine, too, who knew)? They are here, fast wasting away into nothingness? But… What if that other man and his family had been around these parts for quite a long stretch? Had gotten a hand up, and a leg, all the help they would have needed to get themselves sorted out, on the shelf, I beg… "True." Got set on their way to prosperity and such, quite unlike how it was to be with you and me, us? What if this other man and his family had just arrived, with hopes, dreams, plans, and a purpose in his heart to become somebody in this land, just because he hasn't gotten there yet? Although in their head and heart, in their actions and behavioral patterns, too, yes, those parts. They were already there, so much so that they'd got you fooled into thinking that they had already arrived on the money street, and it was your turn to come and take your share of what that man and his family had achieved. When, in fact, they weren't at that place yet? Does that then make it okay to want to toss that man's child (or his children there, all of them) up under the bus? Just because he hasn't arrived on the money street, yet, as you'd supposed and thought? Could it be that these things are happening to you and yours, around you and your doors every single day? I'm talking to the others of you onlookers now, okay? Could all these things be going on around you constantly, but you can never see them? The same as how you could never see anything else, not even me, Cliff, and his wee men? Could it possibly be? But then again, what do I know? Just asking, Bro.

But what if the money we didn't have to give you were the things you were after from the start and wanted to pursue? But you're just now finding out the real truth, that we had not gotten there yet, my youth, as you thought? So, now it's high time to toss us up under the blinking bus because the things that you wanted most from us, from the start. You're more than sure now that we ain't got it. If it were all that easy, though, to get one's hands on all that Doe, as you'd thought and supposed. Why do you still have your empty hands outstretched in front of your nose? Open and turn up to receive all the time, from the plates, even, and never receiving, nor giving a dime, ever. Even after being here in a land of plenty for the same amount of time, still running on empty and eying mine? Yet, because that man and his family haven't gotten it yet either, even though (unlike you) they had just arrived at your door, on the meager. Do they deserve to be tossed, headlong, under the blinking bus?

This might be a good place to insert a piece of spoken word poetry for you from the man himself, Elkhan, the Elk. Or is he... Here goes a poem called.

Ain't even sheet. The friendship poem.

So, is that the way you happen to seeit, that my family and I ain't even sheet? Just because we haven't arrived at the money street, yet? While you were already there, busily lifting loads of multicolored discrete, off the other folks' bundle of joy, and sorrows too, pick-a-booboo.

Joy was brimming with laughter while crying, too. Shedding tears of yet more joy, and bouncing baby boy, and girls, in dancing ballerina shoes, who do you...? That was just because you had happened to discover that my family and I haven't yet crossed over.

Over the bridges and turnstiles, turning the corner. That's where Wall Street's big shots' money garnered was to show you that my family and I ain't even squat. Because we haven't yet got, like, got it all backed up to the loading dock,

In trucks and backhoes, backed up with all that; doe, ray, me, fah, so, yet. Like you'd thought in afterthoughts long, long ago, when you had set out to become and became a friend. To me and my children, but then again.

Your plans were thwarted when the doe that you wanted wasn't forthcoming, coming, coming. And the friendship began a-doning, downing, doning, downing, done.

Chapter nineteen

S ome Other Kinds of People, Though.
  In his capacity as a school bus driver, Elkhan the elk would have happened to be assigned a route beside her. Which was to see him transporting some other kind of kid, of another kind of people, quite unlike these, regularly. He remembers it well. One day, while driving along with the slow-moving traffic. Twenty or more passengers were on board his vehicle and rocking in the pocket. This girl broke away from the chatter in the bus, yes, the hot pan. She pulled down a window and shouted to the teenage boy... Come on, yes, he was walking along the sidewalk at the time, alongside a slow-moving line of traffic, on the way to the park. The girl shouted it at the boy, calling him by name and giggling with joy. "I love you," she said, and the compliment was returned, back to her head. "I love you, too." Quite casually, it was said. Everyone continued doing as they were before, going ahead, on their way to gracing the shore, Miss Mildred. From the Elk's observation, no one at all, whether inside or outside the bus, even on the ball, whooping the toss, or out on the street, the sidewalk, or anywhere else around the park. No one seemed to blink an eyelid a little bit faster. So, what's the point here? Did you ask her? What are you saying? I heard you, yes, all of you asking those questions, you bet. But allow me to "Word you" a bit. The point here is this: from where we're coming, we as a people. In our neck of the woods (and yours, too), I'm sure. Well, unless you happen to be the one walking there on the floor, the one we were addressing before. One would be stretched to breaking point, to hear of anything like that; one

would be far more likely to hear something quite the opposite, to spot the joint. Or even worse than that. Like, something more or less like; hey, Bram, or whatever else the name might be, or become. You... I hate you, I'mma gonna kick your blessed assurance too. Or even worse. You're a dead man, Brad. I'm gonna kill you, he might curse. Laughs, laughs, everybody is laughing, because... yeah! Because they're glad, with the half-spring, and if someone, some nerd or weirdo from somewhere. Like this other kind of kid walking there, just for example, my dear, if he should have happened to be anywhere near this latter bunch, over here. Or even where you are and should have inadvertently said those words; those same, rather beautiful words, like those that were exchanged between the two young kids, from another ethnic group, we'd so heard, other than our kind. But within earshot of this bunch of our own, and dying. He would stand a good chance of getting himself beaten to a pulp. Or get laughed at to scorn, at the very least of the bone.

"Different socialization," you say to these at home? Yeah, I heard you, but really now, if you're a forward-thinking, caring, progressive kind of person, and daring. Let me "word you" with an ask... or two. Which of the two groups would you rather be in, and why can't the one be, or be made to become (in some ways) like me, I mean, like the other?

On another occasion, the Elk was found doing the same sort of tasks for them. No, not like, not for anything more than an amen, no. But for the other ones, for payment, driving home a group of mostly teenagers from school on the bus, as per the agreement. Another school, this time, with teenagers of another racial background than his and mine. But more of the kinds we spoke about earlier, at top speed, I ain't lying. Out the window again, the girl was to stick her head and shout at the teenage boy who was there playing tossed balls on the plains, or the playing field, grass high, and haying. "Hey," she said, "Wanna make babies with me?" And the Elk was like, "How come no one ever asked me that?" From within himself, of course. But we all do know the answer. We've always known the answer. Even when we didn't know that we knew those answers, we knew that one, Sir. Some things are very taboo in our neck of the woods, and our homes, and to think that our folks, chiefly our church folks and the goods, (half-boned) like to poke all sorts of fun at these types of folks, saying things like, "They're still waiting for the Messiah to come." We say it all the time, don't go lying now and deny that one. "They're still waiting for the Messiah; that's why they have so many children." Or, every one of these women thinks that her child is going to be the Messiah. Laughs, and yet more laughs. "You liar." But again, perhaps. You do know what foo... I mean, those other faraway people like you. You know what they do best, don't you? They make a mock at sin and other such things, oh, *what a sin ting*! Or was it something? Meanwhile, these people tell the young ones amongst themselves, and in style, wait... "Wait on the Lord," they say, for the children, or for the child to go and play the games of the day. As the years come and go away again, carrying the best years of those young ones' lives with them, and the very thing that would, could, and should ensure that that thing for which they are waiting and praying fast, (to get married and start a family, in high class). The best of their childbearing years, the family-creating years. Those things are fast slipping away from them, and theirs. Because, as a people, we're so over-tabooed with the whole idea of sex, sexuality, and having babies. So much so that we lay waste somewhere in the waist indeed, I mean, West Indies. We even despise the very words, it would seem. We have seen and heard it way too often; the way some of our folks would react to questions, or any arguments surrounding said subjects, asked of them, even married women from among us. Should someone dare to inquire about when the babies will be forthcoming, after they have gotten married, for example, and humming? Like normal people the world over tend to do. This is the response one is likely to get from our folks and you. It's likely to be some pushback of some sort or spew. "What kind of nastiness are you asking me? *Yuh gweh fram mi yah.*" Yes, I-yah, (kiss mi dyam teet). Oh no, my teeth hurt. It's not those other people, though, those people who do everything as a community and as a people. They're the ones who are getting things to happen in the world, the real world, that is. But they are still the tail, the nobodies, right? We, on the other hand, have been serving them well. Going and coming, in and out of their houses, serving them, seeing and hearing things, and hastening to go and tell. Telling tales, but never learning Nuttn. Or even "anything" worth learning. And yet, what can those folks or anyone else do to stop us from being the head? "Absolutely nothing," they have said. It's just our portion, just the way things are, and that's that, Mi Bred. Pinto finale.

Those folks have a history, too, you know, not unlike our history in some regards, to show you... But they have risen above it, and we have not. I wonder why, why not? Could it be because we're not too big on the "history" thing either? Be it his story or mine, to please her? Not our story, though, that's for sure. Other than to *"pop tory gimme," maybe, so I can have a good time laughing and then, goh get a belly full and goh li dung anh sleep.* Or go to bed, lie down, and sleep, like how those folks like to say it out there on the street. I know you wanna laugh, so go right on, laugh a kikikikikee. Let them stroke your funny bones, mi pickney, all the way home, with me. You must be pampered, like the sweet and cuddly little kids that you are, in the hamper. The real kids, even, of the ram kind, Sir. Kids who like to jump on the rocks and prance all about on time or all day long, no doubt, and into the evening. Not a care in the world, nothing to worry about, nor the girl who deceives me, with the words from her mouth. Nothing hard for you. So, close this book, and go instead to the other book; the social type of book. Now, take a look, and let them lie to you there. Or tell you the truth, they were to hear, the ugly truth, beware. Or even the beautiful and the cute. Which all of you already know anyway, like, how beautiful you are today, as always, and never anything other than... The same as how they will tell those "Others" their truths too, from the gut, even. You know them, the ugly ones, you see them there all the time. Everybody knows that they are ugly, no denying, and they? They know it too. So, there's nothing to it when others tell them what they already know, right? Just like you, the beautiful ones, and the bright... There's nothing to it, it's just the way thou art.

So, why bother with the hard stuff when life is this easy? Leavey, as in, leave it alone, let it be.

Which of your emotions will win in the end, and rule the day, though? Anger? Or joy, and laughter? As for me, I'll choose to laugh and go laughing at myself. If only to stop me from crying, alone on the shelf.

Chapter twenty

C o-signer, the Debt Trap.

  "Why wait?" they say when you can have it today. So, you grab it like the left hind leg of a rabbit, things are going your way, so you say, no longer running away as before. You feel good, really good, for a while. Because you never had anything like that before, but now you do, you have it in style. Then you saw the neighbors' new shiny stuff, you want that too. You go out and get it, like you already know that you must; who's to stop you? Then one day, the real trouble was to come your way, which is common to all, and which the wise of the earth plan for. Including, but not limited to, your moneylenders. Those who are still there, and are there even now, still planning, wheeling, dealing, and who's still willing and able, too, to bend down and help you out. With the "more money" you need now, and the cravings in your mouth. But you now find that you have already used up something you previously had, but didn't even know that you had it. It's called a credit score, or credit rating, yet some more, today's new habit. You can borrow other people's money, a tiny bit of that "other people's" money, the money you borrow when you don't need it, to buy things you don't need. So funny, sit, sit down, please, and eat. To go out and impress people you don't even like. That would have been because you already knew that they didn't like you, and that's why you didn't care about them either, right, Boo? At the time, too, you swore and boasted about how blessed you were. Told no end of stories about what the Lord has done for you so far, but you now have a regular monthly repayment schedule to honor and to do, so that the man and his children may be fed, perpet-ually, too. If and when you and your spouse can't (together) get them to extend yet more credit to you, because you've both used and messed up that facility. They then tell you, "Yes, you can have it, but you're go-ing to need a co-signer." What this means is you must now go out and find her, go and convince your son, your daughter, your brother, and your sister. Or anyone else in your family circle who has not yet sold her-self out to the devil, mister... sorry, I meant to say, to them. You must get them to come in and join up with you and yours. Shaking hands in agreement, to become enslaved to them, once more. Whatever you do or don't do in this life, take it from this fool here who doesn't know Nuttn. No, not even his wife without the button. Not anything at all. Save yourself the trouble and avoid the fall. Don't do this. Ever.

Since we're on the subject of savings, be it saving yourself from some-thing, or... Well, whatever. Like, saving money, or people out of their perceived predicaments. Here are some more do's and don'ts for you in that regard, of the fence. Do: help people out, if and when you can. Don't; don't make a habit out of helping people out, whether or not you can. Especially, not the very same people all the time. It's not good for either of you, the giver or the receiver of the dime. The old man has something to say on this matter, too. No, not that old man across from you, but another one. This is yet another wise old man, a grand old man from further on. The old man had said one should always reach out and lend a helping hand to a stranger, and the bed. Lend the bed, especially, yes. Especially to strangers because we were once strangers, (to the cross, even) at one point or another, good evening. But don't give him always, don't just give him the food, for instance. But give him the wherewithal to go out and produce or provide his food for himself and his ten sons. For example, just for example, give to the stranger who has just arrived on your doorstep, food to eat and a place to sleep, yes, and the bed too. So that he won't have to go out and beg for food or sleep outside un-der the night dew. If at all, you can. But also give him a chance at start-ing over from scratch, if needed. What it means is this: while you're there feeding the hungry man, don't forget to give him potato seeds also, in his hands. So that he can grow meat plants, along with the mashed potato meal on the plate in his hand, like these, bean seeds, too, for instance. The old man's logic is that you should feed that man for three months, and no longer. That is because, apart from taking care of immediate hunger, you should do for him those things that will last longer. Because if he were to do the right thing with those seeds, by starting his breed. Like, if he had gone out and planted them as he should? They would have been producing food for him that was good by then. You want to be a doer of good deeds, my friends, to the people who are in need, and those whom you feed. But not an encourager or enabler of bad and destructive habits like these.

By the same token, if your friend comes to you and asks you for some funds to put fuel in the car to go out and get things done today, and then some. Like, to get to work and so on. By all means, don't let the person go away, or not be able to leave and go away from your door or anywhere else. That would be just because there is no fuel in the car to enable him to go anywhere whatsoever. Don't let him leave without the money or the fuel, mi Bredda, whichever one you can, on the duel. Unless you absolutely cannot find it anywhere, to give him, yeah, that man, or the fool over there. However, if that said person should come back to you two, three, or four times more asking that very same favor of you, and at your door, knocking on the key, trying to get through. Don't give in, don't give it to him. Let him go and learn how to manage his affairs correctly, to his win. And you, too, need to learn some things. Like, you'd better learn how to say "No" before the community loses both of you down below, the Abyss. The easy rider who will not learn how to be a man (or a woman). He will not spare or deny himself anything, be it a great or small plan. No matter how foolishly and unnecessarily it leaves his hand. Because he knows where to go for help every time. The bleeding-heart do-gooder, also, who will not save himself and those who need to be saved by him, and her. Like his own family, for instance, his seed even. He needs to go and learn some of these things, too. It's him whom they (his spouse and children) are looking to and depending on in the house. To save them against the evil day coming down the roads. Which is bound to get to the point of coming sooner or later, better sooner than later, I suppose. But if he gives in to the con man all the time, be it this one sitting right here on the mime, or the other contrite person over there to find. If he continues along that line unabated. It won't be long before he, too, and even you won't have the wherewithal to help anybody at all, same as he did. Not even his newborn baby, in the crib. Take it from this fool who knows nothing that could be learned in school. He's been there and done that too, too many times. On either side of the Leger here, too, no denying it.

"Thank you" is in order here, again, my friends who have been there for me. In my greatest hours of need. There were many. It's not that I've crossed over and won't see those days again, any. No, not at all. I just decided to approach it all differently and to test the strength of that wild beast in front of me. If only to see what metals he is made of, probably. I won't be taking the easy route out anymore. Because I've learned that, that road sure is not easy for either of us.

But consider this. If the friend or brother whom you'd helped out last week, by putting fuel in the car, like this. Was the same one whom you had helped in like manner, the week before? Now he's coming again this week to ask for more. Like, the same favor from you at your door. What is there to suggest that he won't be coming again next week, for more? And then, when the big-ticket items come up, like, not the gas this time, but the car or the bus, Ted cup cup, cupped-up line. Guess who he will be running to first and foremost? Yep, the same foo... I mean, the same person from whom he already knows that he can get what he'd set out to get. With neither regrets nor long-term debts to pay back, anyway. Will you now obey what I have to say? Don't say nay, whatever you do or don't do, please.

How did we get to this, though? How is it that you have allowed yourself to be talked and taught into a situation like this, where you're now oh so vulnerable? Your very existence is now dependent on the grace and favor of the other man, and the terrible. It was probably when you started listening to them and looking over the fence. That was when we, you, he, and I, stopped doing our kind of things. We stopped acting in ways like those of our grandparents, your great-grandparents, your ancestors, yes, and mine. The way they had acted for thousands upon thousands of years, on their side of the fence, was divine. Which would have brought you, me, and them, yes. Our children, even. It was those things that had managed to bring us thus far. Did we ever think of using the rearview mirror in our bus, Ted car? Do we as a people ever turn around and look behind us? If you have, do you like what you now see on the bus? I mean, do you like what you see? I sure don't.

You cry for help, but none is forthcoming, so you run to your brother or sister, the one you have taken on in recent times, and running to, while humming, always Mister. In the place of your real brother, sister, mother, and father, too. Oh, wait a minute, I forgot, it's not true, not many of those types are left around these parts of the lot tory pots who... No, not for you, none of the father types. Not many of them are floating around in this group. I wonder why? Could it be that those are (or should be) cut from a different piece of cloth, like me? He would have different ways of looking at things by nature and in his thoughts, no? Or at least, if they don't, they probably should, but they may also have a way of rubbing the supplanters the wrong way. The fakers, someone else might say. So, if and when they do come, (the men type)? If and when they come to your churches? They don't usually stay, not for long anyway. It could even be because those, real male types, the father types, are probably supposed to be able to see and think things through, even twice. Think differently than others do, even me, and you. Not like the others, such as supplanters, you and your women do. "Amongst others?"

"Yes, but." Is there someone somewhere with a vested interest in keeping the men out of the lives of the children? Out of the families of a certain kind of people, with the intent of killing them? Our people, mostly? Am I even allowed to ask, you Boasey? Those "other" family members, though, are all you seem to care about over there, no? Oh, it's getting late, so I'm out of here. Go.

Chapter twenty-one

I Want to Pay You Back for Loving Me.

You did listen to me when I was talking all that sheet of nonsense, so listen to me on this, too, whatever you do, or don't do. Be sure to do this.

This is high on the list of things you need to know before going to "foreign," or even shopping, wherever you might happen to go or be. Your credit, for example, be sure to protect it, even with your life, and more, some," for me. This is where we pay you back all the money that you might have paid to buy this book, and with interest, too, multiplied to the thousandth fold for you, not the crooks. If only you would dare to pay attention to what we tell you here and make the necessary adjustments to your ways of doing things, my dear. So come eavesdrop on this conversation, and learn a thing, two, or more. Will you?

These were extracted from some edited version of some phone transcripts that were to have transpired between Elkhan "The Elk" and a financial institution that took place while he was going through those very hard times. Behold, he is now baring his soul, going all out here before you, because he loves you like that and does not wish for you to make the same mistakes, as he did, and does.

Note. Pertinent and identifying pieces of information are omitted here for obvious reasons.

Call recording: Hello, this is Henry. Ah, we have an appointment next week, ah, it'd be very important that you actually get insurance, as we talked about last time, ah, so, once you got a quote and get it going, you can also bring me the copy, let me know, I'll call you back on Tuesday in the office, on Tuesday, Telephone number, (the telephone number was given here) Bye, bye.

Note further. This was transcribed by way of the answering machine. It came in after the next message that will now follow. Bear in mind that this was transcribed from speech; therefore, normal (or abnormal) speech patterns may be reflected here.

This right here (especially the bracketed portion) is the be-all and end-all of what he, as well as the other caller we are about to hear from, had called about. No matter how one may try to spin it or shout. Follow along and learn.

Call recorder transcript #1. The date here is time: 1:25 PM.

Caller: Hello, Mr. Elkhan.

Elkhan: Yes, speaking.

Caller: How are you?

Elkhan: OK, you?

Caller: Good, good. Ah, tell me, for our appointment... policy for the house, please.

Elkhan: The what?

Caller: Can you make sure you bring the insurance policy for the house?

Elkhan: I don't have any coverage on the house now, and I'm sure that's the reason why you're calling me now.

Caller: What? What did you say?

Elkhan: I do not have any coverage now, and I'm sure that is why you called me. I just spoke to someone else today on that matter, and I told them I don't...

Caller: Yes, but you understand that you have to have one...

Elkhan: I do understand that.

Caller: You have to always have one?

Elkhan: But also understand that there is a situation that I'm currently in, and I'm trying to work myself out of it, OK?

Caller: So, what are we going to do about that? Are you gonna call and get some quotes? Are you going to call and get some quotes?

Elkhan: If I'm...? Interrupted.

Caller: ...coverage, your house has to be insured.

Elkhan: I know that, and as soon as I can, I will. I'm actually driving now, though, and I have 48 people behind me who are watching and seeing me doing the thing that I'm not supposed to do, so, if you can call me back...

Caller: ...like a broker and take care of it? That way, when we meet, we'll have all the papers. OK?

Elkhan: I'll talk to you in ten minutes.

Caller: No problem, bye.

It's all here in this call, folks. Couldn't you just feel it, the apprehension, suspicion, tension, suspense, and more?

So, why did Henry call? Here is the answer, here is why. Someone else had called earlier.

Transcript #2. (The date here), time; 10:34 AM.

Caller: Hello, Mr. Elkhan?

Elkhan: Yes.

Caller: Hi, this is Frederick (not his real name) ...from the bank? How are you?

Elkhan: I'm good, you?

Caller: Hello?

Elkhan: Yes, I'm OK.

Caller: I see, actually, I received a message from you yesterday.

Elkhan: Yes, I'd called in regards to my mortgage. But I also spoke to my agent, and we have an appointment set up.

Caller: (cutting in). Do you have an appointment with him for this October?

Elkhan: Ah, Tuesday coming...

Caller: OK, no problem. Alm, yes, you can do the follow-up with him. Now, on the mortgage, I can see that there is a payment missing, so now we have updated the mortgage payments, it's now $—.67 on account number one (up from $—.00), and on account number... it's...

Elkhan: I saw where... I took a partial statement from the bank machine a couple of days ago, and it showed that a series of withdrawals were made of the said amounts as were stated here. And I'm, I don't quite understand why, because I'm... I have four mortgages there, and that amount, the installments are to be taken out from my checking account periodically, some weekly, some biweekly, and some monthly. I don't quite remember which is which now, but I know that I have weekly, biweekly, and monthly.

So, I don't know why they'd stopped taking it, and then they took all of that money from my account in one shot.

Caller: Ah, let me, let me tell you what happened. It's because... the number one account?

Elkhan: Yes.

Caller: The number one account was due for renewal.

Elkhan: Yes.

Caller: So, it wasn't done on time, so it was renewed automatically, so that's why, alm, once the renewal was made, they took all the past due payments. Now there's only one payment left, so they're gonna take it today.

Elkhan: So, now, this is what I don't quite understand because, like you told me just now, it was renewed automatically when you did that; those things so this is the thing. I've gotten some notices from the bank that said that... well, I can't say which of the accounts it was related to, since I'm on the job now and hence, not at home where my files are, but... I have more than one notice. So I'd assumed that the other accounts were renewed, just like you just said to me now... You said they were renewed automatically. Why then wasn't that one renewed also, in a timely manner, as the monthly... or weekly ones, as the case might have been? Why wasn't that done, ok? So, the thing is, my question here is why? Since, like you'd just told me that this, as it now is, it is renewed, "automatically," why then do I have to go make an appointment with the bank to renew it, when you are here telling me that it is renewed now? And I have other notices now, which tell me that the other accounts were also renewed, in those same ways...

Caller: OK, sir, I spoke to you, actually, several times regarding the renewal. You said you have the confirmation number that you received "with" your advisor.

Elkhan: This is what I'm saying, no, not a number, these were letters that were sent to me. I didn't know who you were when you called and were talking to me.

Caller: I, I called you, I said; I'm Fred from the bank, and that I was calling about your mortgage at...

Elkhan: laughs, laughing.

Caller: I told you it was about your renewal. You told me you have already renewed your mortgage, and I did a follow-up with your advisor, and it wasn't the case.

Elkhan: Sir...

Caller: I told you, if it was not done, it would be automatically renewed, the mortgage interest will be XX%, and that's the case right now.

Elkhan: Sir, I...

Caller: You have an appointment with your advisor, you can do the renewal with him and then, ah...

Elkhan: I am not sure if you are hearing yourself right now, because if you are here telling me that, actually, what you are telling me, and ah, what you said there? When the scammers are calling people up, they are going through the exact same sorts of things. It's hard to differentiate who is legit from who is fraud when they are calling and telling you things, so some things I don't do on the phone, OK? And if I have written things (correspondences) in my files that say to me: your mortgage is renewed, and such and such are the new terms, and then I'm having people calling me up, people whom I do not know, and cannot say from whence they came, but they are calling, and telling me things that... look, I have been there before, I have been through it, and I do not do those sorts of things anymore ok? When people are calling and telling you things, they are telling you, quite convincingly, things that ah, it's so, and I... you are there telling me that my mortgage is not renewed, while I have correspondence from my bank that says it is so, it is renewed, I'd much rather to go along with what I'm getting from my bank. So, until...

Caller: Hold on, I, I, I honestly understand your concerns, so, whenever you receive a phone call, if you're not sure if it is scam or not, the thing to do is, do the follow-up with your branch, you either call them or you pass by your branch. You can't just receive a call and not sure if it's a scam or not, and just not do anything about it. And I think I sent you a letter, you said you received a letter notice?

Elkhan: And I told you that, I said, I have more than one notices that said the mortgage is renewed, that's why I doubted the person who was calling and talking to me, someone who I didn't know, and I talked to my agent last week or some time ago, and that was when he told me that... actually, I was in the process of trying to renew, get my mortgage renewed, shifting my mortgage from this bank to get it renewed somewhere else. That was when I realized that something was going on, and I think that that is what is causing everybody to be panicking and doing all these things, in effect, pushing me down in a deep hole, because something is on my account, which I am right now in the process of contesting. (If that's the correct term for it), because this is an issue that has shown up now. I got my files from Trans Union, and I realized this, and I am in the process of working on it, so... When I started that process. Henry called me, and I talked to him. That was when I realized it... He told me that one of my many mortgages... I think I have four mortgages there, and one was outstanding to be renewed. So, my question again is this. Why were two or three renewed automatically, and I got those notices to verify, but one was not, and is now causing all of these troubles? And then, somebody is going to go into my account and, according to my partial statement, which I took from the bank machine. Seven withdrawals were made from the account. It could have even been more, but that's what the partial statement showed me. Seven payments were taken out all at once. So, "You could as well die if you like, but I am not leaving a penny in your account." This is the message that was sent to me there. I do not like the way how I'm being treated by my bank... that I've been with for over twenty years. I spoke with another agent that I had there at the bank. Someone whom I don't ever want to be dealing with again, and he told me (among other things), he said, he "doesn't give a shit." This was when I started looking elsewhere to re-move my mortgages, OK? Because I do not like the way how I'm being treated by the bank that I've been with for over twenty years. It's not fair for me, a working man, to be treated this way. In one day, seven or more withdrawals were taken from my account, which... I never gave anybody any directives to go and stop taking the withdrawals from my account in a timely way. No stoppage was put on the other three accounts that I have there.

Caller: I, I, I understand your concerns, OK? But I, I'll, just make sure, you understand, actually, ah, the bank? If you are... on your mort-gage, or for your visa. If you are two months late and you have the money available in the accounts. The bank has the right to take the money from your account.

Elkhan: Yes, I understand that.

Caller: ...because, if you owe two months late... on your visa? It's affecting your credit score, affecting your credit bureaus, which means your mortgage will be affected. Your mortgage interest will be raised, and it will cost you more on your mortgage. Now, with the visa account. I can see that you are over the credit limit, and that is something that we'll discuss later on.

Elkhan: But I'm... all of these actions serve to do that, because. When you, my bank, does these things and I am... Let's say I get a bounced check for insufficient funds, and you are then charging me $65.00 more on top of each and every one of those. I'm coming much faster out of the hole that you are digging for me, right? Because...

Caller: Hold on. What you've got to understand. This is non-nego-tiable; you are aware of that. If the money is not in your account, you'll be charged. The thing to do is, you've got to make sure that... if you are on a monthly or a weekly payment. Just make sure that the money is there every month or every week. In the account to avoid that situation. And for your concern. I spoke with someone, I don't know if it's your wife, on... (The date here). At 11:24, I spoke with that person. The person said that Alm, her husband, is in charge of it. I guess it is your spouse, I don't know. I spoke to her, she said that she would give you the message, OK? So, I spoke to you at 11:29. You said you don't have any contact with your advisor for now. I gave you the number, and I told you you weren't renewed, for now. So, you should have done the follow-up with your advisor.

Elkhan: Sir, sir, I'm sorry to be cutting in, but I'm at work, and I have to go very shortly. So, I don't know if we can continue this, but...

Caller: Listen, just do the follow-up with your advisor. You said you have an?

Elkhan: I have an appointment with him...

Caller: Definitely. For now, let me tell you what will happen. There is two mortgage payments late, the system will take it today. So, the system will take two mortgage payments from your account just to keep it up to date. The amounts... $ ...And on your Visa? Just to let you know that you are over the credit limit to the tune of... $

Elkhan: Sir, I know all of that, and again, you have nothing to do with this but I'm going to tell you what is going on. You said you spoke to my wife the other day. (Or it could have been someone else, but let's just say "wife," for the sake of making the point). My wife is... look. If you are there digging me into a hole. You, whom I don't know, and my wife in my house is doing the exact same thing? I called the credit card office the other day because I'm seeing these things, purchases on my report or statement that I don't know anything about, and he told me where to call to investigate it. That's when I realized, it's "my wife" who is taking... Going behind my back and buying things with my credit card, which I didn't give her permission to do, and which I have no knowledge of. I did not know that any of these things were going on, and I do not have the money to pay for it. So, whatever happens is gonna happen, but. I'm in a pickle and I really, really have to go now and... I'm a bus driver and...

Caller: No problem, do the follow-up with your advisor, he will tell you what to do, for now. Oh, can you confirm before you go? Is there insurance on the house right now? Is it insured?

Elkhan: No, sir, it's not insured.

Caller: No? What happened? Exactly? What, why is it not insured?

Elkhan: As I have said, Sir, I have to go, I am telling you. I'm in a pickle, and if I cannot, if you are there taking money from my account and leaving me with not a penny in there, plus giving me an additional sixty-five dollars for every action. It is pulling me into a deep hole that I cannot get out of, and there are things that I'm going to have to cut, and that insurance is now cut for the time being, I can't afford it, OK?

Caller: It does not work like that, sir; you need to have insurance on the house.

Elkhan: Well, I need to have money to have it, sir. I do not have the money now. I am taking austerity measures in trying to work my affairs out, OK?

Caller: If there's no insurance on the property, Sir, the bank will take legal action, OK?

Elkhan: Well, they will have to do that and put me in yet a deeper hole again, and then everything will go. I cannot do any more, sir. My bank who is supposed to be there to help me, is digging a hole for me. My wife in my house is digging, everybody around me who is supposed to be there for me... to support me is doing the exact same thing. I cannot do it anymore, ok?

Caller: Well, this is... there's nothing that we can do about it.

Elkhan: Exactly, that's what I'm saying too. You are there who have the power to just go in and take out 8–10 or however much, as much from my bank account, one time, and you are saying that there is nothing that you can do. Now, you tell me, what can I do?

Caller: Talking... Still talking while I'm here talking?

Elkhan: Sir, I have to go, my passengers are here, and they're breathing down my neck. I really have to go now.

Caller: Yeah, I'll do a follow-up with your advisor about this. I I thank you, Sir.

Elkhan: Alright. The follow-up did happen.

Chapter twenty-two

The Analysis.

Here now is where I give my take on the whole thing, for your benefit. In preparation for my analysis, to give you some actionable pointers that you will be able to use in your everyday lives, I need to tell you something about the outlines of the transcript.

Apart from the fact that this was edited somewhat from the original state, to cut and clear away some of the clutter, to protect some very sensitive information and individuals. These are cuttings that, although they did not alter the story any... Some of them did hamper the flow somewhat at times. Secondly, wherever you might happen to come across something bracketed () in this transcript. Just the part relating to the conversation with the banker (no more, no less). They were not part of the transcript. Just comments added on by the narrator as we go along. There may be some underlined pieces too. These are portions of the script or our comments that we found to be very important and should invite closer attention. Finally, from this point on through to the end of the comments on this particular subject. Some statements, questions, and such may be in italics. Those will be some further, more detailed comments, explanations, and instructions in some cases. Designed to guide you, "the readers," away from falling into some of the many pitfalls that are there lurking in the dark, waiting to devour the unsuspecting many, such as you and me.

Here now is our attempt at simplifying the whole thing, so that you (my people) may be able to understand it better. After all, where can our people go to get financial education, such as this? Here is the story, as taken from the call recorder transcript, as transpired between them, the callers, and Elkhan.

Call recorder transcript 1b. Date here. The time: 1:25 PM.

Caller: Hello, Mr. Elkhan.

Elkhan: Yes, speaking.

Caller: How are you?

Elkhan: OK, you?

Caller: Good, good. Ah, tell me, for our appointment. (Some muffled words) ...policy for the house, please. Elkhan: The what?

Caller: Can you make sure you bring the insurance policy for the house?

Elkhan: I don't have any coverage on the house now, and I'm sure that's the reason why you're calling me now.

Caller: What? What did you say? (No, you're not surprised, you already knew that before you'd called, that's one of the reasons why, as a matter of fact).

Elkhan: I do not have any coverage now, and I'm sure that is why you called me. I just spoke to someone else today on that matter (just a short while ago, in fact) ...and I told them I don't...

Caller: Yes, but you understand that you have to have one. (As long as your house is carrying a mortgage, to ensure that, no matter what happens, they will get paid, whether or not you do).

Elkhan: I do understand that.

Caller: You have to always have one...

Elkhan: But also understand that there is a situation that I'm currently in, and I'm trying to work myself out of, OK?

Caller: So, what are we going to do about that? Are you gonna call and get some quotes? Are you going to call and get some quotes? (So, it's "we" who are going to have to do something about it. But it's "you," meaning Elkhan in this case, who is going to have to make those calls, get those quotes, and pay for them too).

Elkhan: If I'm... interrupted.

Caller: ...coverage, your house has to be insured.

Elkhan: I know that, and as soon as I can, I will, I'm actually driving now though, and I have 48 (or more passengers) people behind me who are watching and seeing me doing the thing that I'm not supposed to do, (talking on the phone while driving), so if you can call me back?

Caller: (fading back in) ...like a broker and take care of it? That way, when we meet, we'll have all the papers, OK? (Don't you get the feeling, though, that this here, the insurance? It is the only reason why they, both this one as well as the other guy. The only reason they want to meet with you after all of this is to make sure that the insurance on the house is in good order, so that they can see the real evidence of it. If you haven't yet gotten that notion, you will soon. And why so much emphasis on the insurance? I will tell you what I think by the end of this piece. Perhaps).

Elkhan: I'll talk to you in ten minutes.

Caller: No problem, bye. (Yes, there is a problem, you know it, I know it, and now everybody knows it. You're probably just there trying to smooth the guy over, so he won't know how deeply in ...it, he is. But...).

It's all here in this call, folks. Couldn't you just feel it, the apprehension, suspicion, tension, and suspense? The call came mere minutes after the Elk was done talking to the other guy about the whole mess with the mortgage and all.

So, why did Henry call? Here is the answer, here is why. The other guy had called some moments earlier. (The date omitted here) The time: 10:34 AM.

Caller: Hello, Mr. Elkhan?

Elkhan: Yes.

Caller: Hi, this is Frederick (not his real name) from the bank. How are you?

Elkhan: I'm good, you?

Caller: Hello? (Seems as if he wasn't hearing clearly).

Elkhan: Yes, I'm OK.

Caller: I see, actually, I received a message from you yesterday.

Elkhan: Yes, I'd call in regard to my mortgage. (The Elk had returned a call a day earlier). But I also spoke to my agent, and we have an appointment set up.

Caller: (cutting back in). You have an appointment with him for this October?

Elkhan: Ah, Tuesday coming.

Caller: OK, no problem. (Yes, there are, problems a-plenty, you just wait, you'll see). Um, yes, you can do the follow-up with him. Now, on the mortgage, I can see. (Picture him there with his pile of papers, and foraging through), that there is a payment missing, so now we (we who)? ...have updated the mortgage payments, it's now $ — .67 on account number one, (up from $ — — — .00). And on account number? No. (We'll only be focusing on number one for this lesson. It is the biggest and most important of them all). ...It's...

Elkhan: I saw where... I took a partial statement from the bank machine a couple of days ago, and it showed that a series of withdrawals were made of... (The said amounts as were stated here, above). And I'm, I don't quite understand why, because I'm... I have four mortgages there, and that amount, the installments are to be taken out from my checking account periodically, some weekly, some biweekly, and some monthly. I don't quite remember which is which now, but I know that I have weekly, biweekly, and monthly. So, I don't know why they'd stopped taking it, and then they took all of that money from my account in one shot. (We'll tell you why, as we see it. This one will probably make the biggest bang in impacting their ultimate objectives, probably. Because that was the biggest of the four loans, the one on which the installments were also the biggest. The Elk was trying to play smart with this approach: by paying weekly instead of monthly, as some folks do. One stands a good chance of saving quite a pretty penny over the long run on those mortgage repayments, in so doing. A bit more of the money from those payments is likely to go towards paying down the real debt balance, instead of interest only, or mostly. Remember this, too: some months carry five weeks, and that fifth payment is likely to go mostly towards paying down the debt. Now, consider further, if you, as a common everyday Joe, should have found that out. What is the likelihood that the bankers know it too? No need to worry, though, since the banks are there to look out for your best interest and only yours, right? They don't have any vested interest in having you there paying them the most money they can choke out of you, and for as long as possible, no, not at all. Furthermore, they would never deliberately set out to use snide and underhanded means to try to hold on to a paying customer for a day longer than is necessary. Right)? "Right."

Caller: Ah, let me... Let me tell you what happened. It's because the number one account?

Elkhan: Yes.

Caller: ...The number one account was due for renewal.

Elkhan: Yes.

Caller: So, it wasn't done on time, so it was renewed automatically. (By whom, who was it that had gone in and renewed it now, and why now, but not then)? ...so, that's why, um? Once the renewal was made. (By whom was never told, at least not verbally. But I have my strong suspicions as to who it was that had done it. ...they took all the past-due payments. Who are those "they" of which you speak? Could it be you, sir? But wherever and whenever it becomes convenient, you switch around the pronouns and hence the personage of the individual. To defray the responsibilities from one person or non-person to the other? Perhaps). Continuing... Now there's only one payment left, so they're gonna take it today. (Not you, and certainly not right now, even as we speak. It's not because you are sitting there looking at the account and seeing that there is now enough money in there to meet those payments, it's not that at all, and it's "they" who are going to take it, not you, and it's sometime today, not now, right)?

Elkhan: So, now, this is what I don't quite understand because, as you told me just now, it was renewed automatically when you did that; those things. (They took all the past-due payments, all except one or two, and that was only because there was no more money left there from which to take it or do anything else, not for them, not for the elk. No money was left there, none at all). ...so, this is the thing. I have gotten some notices from the bank which said that, well I can't say which of the accounts it was related to, since I'm on the job now and hence, not at home where my files are but, I have more than one notices, so I'd assumed that the other accounts were also renewed, (One could have assumed under those circumstances that all of the accounts would have been treated in like manner, couldn't she)? ...just like you just said to me now, you said they were renewed automatically. Why then wasn't that one renewed also, in a timely manner, as the monthly or weekly one, as the case might have been? Why wasn't that done, OK? (Could it be that this was a common practice by this and other such institutions, so designed to fleece the unsuspecting customer of everything that they've got? Even that which one may get sometime in the future? I have my suspicions). So, the thing is, my question here is why, since, like you'd just told me that this, as it now is, it is renewed, automatically, why then do I have to go make an appointment with the bank to renew it, when you're here telling me that it is renewed now? (To make sure that they always have a current agreement with your very current signature on it always, probably? They will want to sell you some more nothing when you get there, too. That's how they trap and keep you trapped, don't you know? Pens and paper do it). And I have other notices now, (the conversation continued) which tell me that the other accounts were also renewed, in those same ways.

Caller: OK, Sir, I spoke to you... (This is it right here, the prepared script). ...actually, several times regarding the renewal. (Who is counting, you asked? He is, and he's documenting every tiny detail. That's how it is done in their world, to keep the likes of you and me enslaved and to serve them, always. And the laws, their laws that they, yes, them and their friends make, for this and like purposes, serve them well in getting it done, into perpetuity). You said you have the confirmation number that you received with ("from" is the word I think he had intended, instead of "with) ...your advisor. (I said no such thing, at no time).

Elkhan: This is what I'm saying, no, not a number, these were letters that were sent to me. I didn't know who you were when you called and were talking to me.

Caller: I, I called you, I said I'm Fred, from the bank, and that I was calling about your mortgage at...

Elkhan: laughs. (The Elk had to laugh. "Why?" Wait a minute, you'll soon get to see why).

Caller: I told you it was about your renewal. You told me you have already renewed your mortgage, and I did a follow-up with your advisor, but it wasn't the case. (All of this came out of his prepared script. Picture him there, going through the files; he has it all recorded for future reference if need be. For court lawsuits, too, if need be. Everything is documented in writing and taped recordings, even the times when he'd called you. Down to the milliseconds of the minute. As opposed to you and me, who have nothing to fall back on in such situations, because... We never did bother to write anything down for our records; we only love records of the musical types, and not much more. But he knows and prepares himself. He knows that he might need to prove some things in front of a court of law, in the not-too-distant future. Like, when we'll be there as they try to take the "blessings," sorry, I meant to say, the house from you, from me, from us. So, he prepares himself for that day. But as for you and me? ...well, what-ev-ver).

Elkhan: Sir...

Caller: I told you, if it was not done, it would be automatically renewed, the mortgage interest will be xx%, and that's the case right now.

Elkhan: Sir, I...

Caller: You have an appointment with your advisor, you can do the renewal with him and then, ah. (Notice anything? Notice the change in tone and mode? His work is done in his mind. Except for one more thing, or two, maybe).

Elkhan: I am not sure if you are hearing yourself right now, because, if you are here telling me that, actually, what you are telling me, and ah, what you said there? When the scammers are calling people up, they are going through the exact same sorts of things (similar processes) ...it's hard to differentiate who is legit from who is fraud, when they (the scammers) are calling and telling you things. So, some things I don't do on the phone, OK? And if I have written things (correspondences) in my files that says to me: your mortgage is renewed, and such and such are the new terms, and then I'm having people calling me up, people whom I do not know, and cannot say from whence they came, but they are calling, and telling me things which... look, I have been there before, I have been through it, and I do not do those sorts of things anymore OK? When people (the scammers) are calling and telling you things, they are telling you, quite convincingly, things that ah, it's so, and I? you are there telling me that my mortgage is not renewed, while I have correspondence from my bank that says it is so, it is renewed, I'd much rather go along with what I'm getting from my bank. So, until...

Caller: Hold on, I, I (Here, the human was to come alive in him, if only for a brief moment) ...I honestly understand your concerns, so, whenever you receive a phone call, (really? Every time? He must have meant something else). ...if you're not sure if it is a scam or not, the thing to do is, do the follow-up with your branch, you either call them or you pass by your branch. (Oh, so that was what you meant, as far as it relates to you and what you do, to get paid? Lots of payments for you and your cronies, like the banks, forever? That's what you meant? As long as I'd borrowed the bank and her friend's money, if I get a call saying it's the bank calling, I must then do the following to make very sure, because the onus is always on me from that borrowing day onwards. I see. Now I know and I'mma sure gonna tell my friends, peradventure they might learn, too). "You can't just receive a call and not (be) sure if it's a scam or not, and just not do anything about it." (Yes, I can, at least I could, before I'd permitted you to own me. This is what I want my people to learn from this, if nothing else. How did I, how did we as a people get to this part? I'll tell you. It's in situations like these, where we go a-begging and a-borrowing to buy and consume things; things we don't need, most of the time, at the very least). ...And I think I sent you a letter, you said you received a letter notice?

Elkhan: And I told you that, I said, I have more than one notice that said the mortgage is renewed, that's why I doubted the person who was calling and talking to me, (about the mortgage renewals) someone who I didn't know, and I talked to my agent last week or some time ago, and that was when he told me that... actually, I was in the process of trying to renew, get my mortgage renewed, shifting my mortgage from this bank to get it renewed somewhere else. That was when I realized that something was going on, and I think that that is what is causing everybody to be panicking and doing all these things, in effect, pushing me down in a deep hole, because something is on my account, something that I am right now in the process of contesting (if that's the correct term for it), because this is an issue that showed up now. I got my (credit) files from Trans Union, and I realized this, and I am in the process of working on it, so. When I started that process, Henry called me, and I talked to him (because, Henry, might have noticed the activities on my Trans-Union or other such credit records. They are constantly watching and monitoring it. He might have noticed that I was shopping around for a new mortgage at other institutions, too. So, in monitoring it, they would have gotten to see that. Same as they'll be watching yours after they grab hold of you, that's why he'd called, perhaps). ...that was when I realized it, he told me that one of my many mortgages, I think I have four mortgages there, and one was outstanding to be renewed. So, my question again is this: why were two or three renewed automatically, and I've got those notices to verify, but one was not, and is now causing all of these troubles? (I have my suspicions as to the reasons why) ...And then, somebody is going to go into my account and, according to my partial statement that I took from the bank machine, seven withdrawals were made from the account; it could have even been more, but that's what the partial statement showed me, seven payments were taken out all at once. So, you could as well die (from wants) if you like, but I am not leaving a penny in your account. This is the message that was sent to me there. I do not like the way how I'm being treated by my bank, which I've been with for over twenty years. I spoke with another agent that I had there at the bank, someone whom I don't ever want to be dealing with again, and he told me, among other things, that he doesn't give a shit. This was when I started looking elsewhere to remove my mortgages, and all other businesses from there, (to another place, perhaps, where they do give a shi... I mean, where they do care). OK? I do not like the way how I'm being treated by the bank that I've been with for over twenty years, and it's not fair for me, a working man (or anyone else, for that matter), to be treated this way. In one day, seven or more withdrawals were taken from my account, which... I never gave anybody any directives to go and stop taking the withdrawals from my account in a timely way; no stoppage was put on the other three accounts that I have there. (Not by me).

Caller: I, I, I understand your concerns, ok? (Human again, maybe) but I, I'll, just make sure, you understand, actually, ah, the bank, if you are on your mortgage, (skipping and jumping from place to place, searching for words to chase, I wonder why. Yes, I'm on a mortgage. That's what we've been talking about here, remember)? ...or for your visa, if you are two months late and you have the money available in the accounts, the bank has the right to take the money from your account? (Yes, that may be so, but we were not talking about the visa here, not yet. So, why did he jump from the mortgage that we were talking about at the time, to go on to refer to the visa? Legalities, perhaps. As I've said before, this person is working with written rules, records, and recordings. He is following legal guidelines; whatever he says or doesn't say must be able to stand up in a court of law. He, therefore, had to jump from the mortgage that he was talking about at the time, to then go on to refer to the visa because... The mortgage probably doesn't have such a clause, which states that if the payments are two months late and the money is in the account, they have the right to go in and take it out. But the visa does. Probably, and since that is the said clause that he (seemingly) was using to make those actions, and which he is now also using again, and talking about it, and recording the conversations too. He had to protect himself by switching from the current subject (the mortgage) to add the other (the visa), which he did go on to say that: we will be talking about "later." Not yet, though. Why the switch from one to the other? To protect himself as he goes about squeezing the money out of you ...my brother, that's why).

Elkhan: Yes, I understand that.

Caller: Because, if you owe two months late, on your visa, (again, he has to make sure to say: on your Visa, but that doesn't necessarily mean that it's the same with the mortgage, however, this is the clause that he intends to use against you to get you to make good on the mortgage. This is how they do it, chap. Real smooth). ...it's affecting your credit score, affecting your credit bureaus, which means your mortgage will be affected, your mortgage interest will be raised, and it will cost you more on your mortgage. (So now he is your angel of mercy, saving you money is what he is about now? Yeah, right). Now, with the visa account. (This is where the Visa was set to get discussed, from the start. It just got itself inserted where it was most conveniently needed, then). I can see that you are over the credit limit, and that is something that we'll discuss later on. (Yes, like you've got it all laid out there in your script, it should have been later on, not yet. Same as how you also have the insurance questions on the list. Probably the very last question to be asked before you are done, as it has become the custom with you).

Elkhan: But I'm... all of these actions serve to do that, because when you, my bank, do these things, and I am... Let's say I get a bounced check for insufficient funds, (which was likely what they did for those other two payments, those he said were outstanding too, we'll see when the next monthly statement comes in). ...and you are then charging me $65.00 more on top of each and every one of those, I'm coming much faster out of the hole that you are digging for me, right? Because...

Caller: Hold on. What you've got to understand... (No, that is not what I've got to understand. What I've got to understand, or more like, go back to understanding is this: how to live within my means, like we as a people used to do, and stop borrowing money from people like you. People who love that thing so very much and will do any and everything to get more, much more of it. Even when you've already got more of it than you and every last member of your family on every side could ever exhaust in ten million lifetimes. That is what my kind of people need to understand). ...This is non-negotiable, (he continued) you are aware of that. (Am I? Again, when did you sit me down and tell me this? How are you then to be so sure that I'm aware of this? Or is that just the normal way of doing things in your neck of the woods, where you go around saying things you want others to say, think, and believe? You say these things as often as possible, and with as much force and authority as you can muster up. You write them somewhere in print so small that no one could ever read them without amplifying them. Then say those things until the hearer starts to believe that it is so, no matter how far from the truth, his truth, those sayings are). ...If the money is not in your account, you'll be charged. The thing to do is, you've got to make sure that, if you are on a monthly or weekly payment, just make sure that the money is there every month or every week. (This is it, folks, the be-all, and end-all of it all). ...in the account to avoid that situation. (I'm sure that's what you'd have me do to avoid those types of situations, among other things, or not. It doesn't matter one way or the other to you personally. You'll be paid. But I sure have got some other ideas now that I plan on employing, soon). And for your concern, I spoke with someone, I don't know if it's your wife, on... (A date here) at the time, 11:24. (Very specific, that's how he gets paid, quite handsomely, I'm sure). ...I spoke with that person, the person said that, um, her husband is in charge of it, I guess it is your spouse, I don't know. (Even after she told you, you still don't know)? More legalities, folks. ...I spoke to her, and she said that she would give you the message, OK? So, I spoke to you at 11:29. You said you don't have any contact with your advisor for now. I gave you the number, and I told you you weren't renewed, for now, so you should have done the follow-up with your advisor. (Why was I not renewed? Just another tool in the toolkit, I suppose, part of the overall strategy to hang on to the cash cow for as long as is humanly possible).

Elkhan: Sir, sir, I'm sorry to be cutting in, but I'm at work, and I have to go very shortly. So, I don't know if we can continue this, but... (You think? There ain't no stopping us now, that's for sure).

Caller: Listen, just do the follow-up with your advisor. You said you have an... (Whatever you do, do this, even after all the doings that have been done, why)?

Elkhan: I have an appointment with him.

Caller: Definitely. For now, let me tell you what will happen. There is two mortgage payments late, the system will take... (I'm sure it's the system; that faceless, nameless thing. It's not you, not at all). So, the system will take two mortgage payments from your account (plus the charges, now or whenever thereafter the funds may become available). ...Just to keep it up to date. (Because nothing else matters in the entire world, but keeping those payments to you and yours, up to date, and coming, coming, coming). The amounts... (He went on to repeat the amounts that were to be paid). And on your Visa, just to let you know that you are over the credit limit to the tune of... (He went on to give the exact amount over the limit).

Elkhan: Sir, I know all of that, and again, you have nothing to do with this, but I'm going to tell you what is going on (anyway). You said you spoke to my wife the other day... (Or whoever that person might have been). My wife is... You are there digging me into a hole, you who I don't know, and my wife in my house is doing the exact same thing, I called the credit card office (of the same bank, his bank) the other day because, I'm seeing these things, purchases on my report, or (Credit card statements) that I don't know anything about, and he told me where to call to investigate it, that's when I realized, it's my wife who is taking? Going behind my back and buying things with my credit card that

I didn't give her permission to do and which I have no knowledge of, I did not know that any of these things were going on, and I do not have the money to pay for it, so whatever happens, is gonna happen, but. I'm in a pickle and I really, really have got to go now and... I'm a bus driver and...

Caller: No problem. (No problem, you say, but until you get to say all that you are here to say, nobody moves). ...do the follow-up with your advisor, he will tell you what to do, for now. (But here is the last thing that must be verified before we go, no matter what). Oh, can you confirm before you go, is there insurance on the house right now? Is it insured? (That right there is the mother question; everything hinged on this, it would seem). Every time he called, that was the last question. Even though the answer was "yes" all of the previous times, it didn't stop him from asking again; it sure wasn't going to this time either. No matter how much the man was telling him that "I'm late," and "my passengers are breathing down my neck." He has to get it sorted out before he, or you, or anyone else gets to leave and go anywhere, unless the man should just hang up on him. Which would have only served to solicit yet more calls coming in from him, the man knew that much. (This must be verified, though).

Elkhan: No, Sir, it's not insured.

Caller: No? What happened, exactly... what, why is it not insured? (Give me some details here. That's going to be much more important than going to get your job done by serving your clientele. So that you may earn the money and therefore be in a better position to be able to pay me what you owe me. No. That part is not that important to me. Not now, not ever because, whatever happens, whatever you do, or don't do, I'll be getting paid. Quite handsomely, I'm sure, but...).

Elkhan: As I have said, Sir, I have to go, I am telling you, I'm in a pickle, and if I cannot, if you are there taking money from my account and leaving me with not a penny in there, plus giving me an additional sixty-five dollars (to pay) for every action, (every bounced check, the bank charges that much. On top of whatever else the other parties to whom the bounced check was made payable will charge you). ...it is pulling me into a deep hole that I cannot get out of, and there are things that I'm going to have to cut, and that insurance is now cut for the time being. I can't afford it, OK?

Caller: It does not work like that, sir; you need to have insurance on the house. (It doesn't work like that, for whom? It has never worked for me or the likes of me, that's for sure. No, it's not the house, he meant that you need to ensure that his, and his kind of friends' money, the money that is wrapped up in the house, is insured. At your expense).

Elkhan: Well, I need to have money to (be able to) have it, Sir. I do not have the money now. I am taking austerity measures in trying to work my affairs out, OK?

Caller: If there's no insurance on the property, Sir, the bank will take legal action, OK? (Yes, the bank, not you. And no, don't get me wrong here, folks, and don't take it lightly, especially you, my folks. What he said here is true; the bank, through its many agencies, will take legal action against you in such cases and take everything away from you. Including the "blessing," I mean, the house. Don't allow that to happen, ever).

Elkhan: Well they will have to do that, and put me in yet a deeper hole again, and then everything will go, I cannot do any more Sir, my bank who is supposed to be there to help me is digging a hole for me, my wife in my house is digging, everybody around me who is supposed to be there for me to support me is doing the exact same thing, I cannot do anymore, ok? (Nobody is there for you, mate, you are on your own). Note: The old man was the one who had said. Ain't nobody there to support you, Chap; they are there to get fat and rich, fleecing you. Every last one of them, on every side, and it's quite obvious that they are reaping massive success at it. So, whatever notions you've got or from wherever you've got them. The notion that someone is there to help you, you'll do well to take them right back. You are on your own.

Caller: Well, this is... There's nothing that we can do about it.

Elkhan: Exactly, that's what I'm saying too, you are there who have the power to just go in and take out 8–10 or however much, (more) as much from my bank account (as you like) one time, and you are saying that there is nothing that you can do, now, you tell me, what can I do?

Caller: Talking. Still talking, while I'm here talking.

Elkhan: Sir, I have to go, my passengers are here, they're breathing down my neck, I really have to go now.

Caller: Yeah, I'll do a follow-up with your advisor about this. I, I thank you, Sir.

Elkhan: Alright. The follow-up did happen.

Banknote, via traditional mail. Why insurance? Note: on the very first occasion when the elk would have missed out on two payments, this was the letter that was to follow. Does one have to be a cynic to start believing that this was a subtle suggestion on the part of the institution, an institution with probably hundreds of years of experience under its belt? Long enough to know and understand how people will think and behave in certain situations? Does one have to be cynical to think that that was a part of the play here, even after having seen and heard the rest of the story thus far? The letter reads.

"Your financial institutions have informed us that you are over sixty days in arrears for your insurance premium payments or mortgage loan payments for the above-mentioned mortgage loan, as stated in the termination of insurance clause found on the insurance certificate, on the reverse side of your application. We have terminated your coverage as of the date..." (Date omitted here).

So, according to the notice, it will take just two consecutive missed payments for that clause to kick in, and hence, your insurance coverage will be gone. But the bank unilaterally suspended your mortgage account for nearly ten weeks, according to what was revealed here in this conversation. That would have been more than enough time to have affected the activation of that clause. Then they call you up repeatedly to ask about the said mortgage and related (other) things, such as insurance. Note: The installments were there all along; they just chose to stop taking them for bureaucratic reasons, well, most of it was. Until they started hitting you hard with those charges. Then, they would have been able to monitor one's reactions and actions taken after all of that (or not taken) to straighten it out. The way one deals with said situations should be more than enough to give the institution the information necessary to know down to the dotting of the "I" and crossing of the "t," where such a person is in their financial affairs, or hers. No? Go. So now the vultures can fly down on the carcass, no?

Hey, you there, listen up and hear. We need to wake up, people, wake up, and shake ourselves out of our slumber. Dreams, they say, are for those who sleep, okay? And we have been slumbering in Titanic mode all week. If we think that a change has come for the better, for progress and such, as some had supposed. We had better think again.

Check out the real situation. When was it, or where was it? Was there anybody, in whatever form that might have been, who came to your rescue? Nobody was out searching for you to help you out and support you, my friend. But one day, it would have finally happened. You became somebody in their world, in their eyes, and in their schemes of things. In their schemes of financial things. That particular day when it happened for them was probably when you were registered by your papa or mom. Or the day when you'd gotten yourself a social number. Or a job, a credit card, and hence a credit score, or the beginning of building a credit score. Maybe one of those days or just before. That was the day, however, when you'd enter into their world, probably. They started watching you, tracking you, and monitoring you. Your activities, that is. Your financial activities, to be precise. Your earning power: income and expenses, and other such things, are nicer to them as it is. To see how much money you have coming in versus how much you are paying out. How well were you making those payouts? Is your income growing, and how fast? And such were the likes, they would have asked. After they had gotten all of those things figured out, they would have been able to make informed projections and predictions, then seek you out aggressively. Make some offers you cannot refuse unless you refuse them.

You would have been wise to refuse those said offers, though, or else. You would then be seen spending a tiny bit of their money, their tainted money, which they would have gotten by these very means, as well as other such schemes and trickery. You will gladly be spending a tiny bit of that on a large pile of junk that you don't need, but just want. Or was made to want by, guess who, and his aunt? Then you become more and more addicted to it all, both the apparent "easy money" and the mountains of junk, until the fall. So much so that it would have blinded your eyes so that you never get to see how much and how easily they had made you a slave again, guys. And me? No. To serve them willingly this time, and into perpetuity. If you are lucky, you get to die happy. Because you would have played your role faithfully, serving them. Paying them the regularly scheduled installments even before every due date, you send. So that you can get a good name and a good credit score. So that you may go out and buy some more and die just as poor as ten thousand generations before. Never having owned so much as a door. Nor leaving for your children's children, even so much as the tusk of a wild boar. Now, when they, the bank, had sent you that letter, teller, shouting and telling you that you were preapproved for that load...? I mean that loan. That handy little piece of cash, spending pounds, in weights and measures. "Blessings," you had called it and laughed, through the mouth hole wide and round, because it was the answer to your prayers that came fast. Yeah, right. Save it to buy another prayer, you are surely going to need it.

Here, then, is my foolish advice to you. Stay away from that man and his ill-begotten gain, no matter how he packages and sells it to you, under whatever name. Whether he chooses to call it a loan (pre-approved loan) or a mortgage. Cash extension and credit cards, line of credit, or whatever else there is to sell it. They're all the same, designed to sell you back into slavery, again. Don't get me wrong, though, there are some things, some good things even. Things that you can do with some of those instruments. Things that could benefit you in the long run (away from them). Home loans, for instance, or business loans, or car loans, to a far lesser extent. But don't ever borrow the man's money in whatever form to go shopping. Not to go on a vacation, or a cruise, and such, not happening. If you can't pay for those upfront, then it means that you can't afford them, those sorts, and since you don't need them. Leave them right there where you'd found them.

Suppose there were a type of people who never did anything, like people who do nothing at all, other than nothing. Like, be born, and then grow up, as is the dictate of nature from then on. Get dragged off to church, to make vows, of varying types, before that one even had a chance to learn the ways and consequences of vows and lies. Learn nothing but nothing. Then go off and break those vows, even in the church. Then make more and go to church again, and sing, and dance, and have a good time. Then go back home and boast about the good times that they have had in the church and communion, fake wine that always quenches their thirst. Then waste away, and die, and go running off to heaven, to do what, may I ask?

23

Chapter twenty-three

The Foundation is Funded and Growing.

Vince had a name; he had the money, cars, girls, everything shiny and new. But then, just like Humpy Dumpty, Vince had a big fall, which was coming to him all along the waterfall. Looking at it all now, one is tempted to believe that that was the plan all along, wow, on the part of someone, yes. Somebody, somewhere, had such plans and dreams; it has always been there, it would seem. The plan was to take the black man's body and muscle and use it to enrich everybody else but him. As in, everyone but the black man within his skin. After that other man was done with the black man and his muscles, he would just discard him as waste among the Brussels. Yes, from among the sprouts, wasted and cast out. But there came a time when that man was forced to pay people back for their labor. Including, but not limited to, the black men, in his favor. They paid him alright, but then quickly got out and formulated plans and schemes to take back that night, all that they had was to pay him to fight, and more.

You see, all that money that Vince made and would then lose to the cast didn't just disappear into thin air towards the corked-on screws, in the bars. It went into someone's pocket, somewhere, among the creators of the tools. Try as you may, you'll be hard-pressed to see anyone from Vince's community today, his family, his neighborhood, even. Anyone at all who is reflecting the evidence of being the benefactor of the spin-offs from all of that money, which once belonged to Vince, and by extension, to them, that's not funny. So, where did the money go? Just asking, Bro. As for Timothy, although they were kinfolks, Tim was cut from quite a different kind of cloth. His reach is enormous and growing every day. It's hard to imagine a scenario where Tim will become irrelevant and fade away, like, from where things are today. Even if by some weird twist of fate, he should drop off the edge of the earth and onto your plate. The impact that he has had on these people can and will remain, for a mighty long time to come, piloting the plane, towards a touchdown. With Timothy's help, Vince has revamped himself... well, so the story goes. He's a motivational speaker of renown these days, and a globetrotter too, of some sort of craze. As far as the church and its leaders are concerned, though, not so much so. Chetalee still supports her local church, her very own. As well as many other churches on dirty grass, yes, look, it's overgrown. Continuing on the journeys, both locally and internationally. As for them, though, as for the churches and what they do (or what they choose not to do), they're still there getting along by putting one foot in front of the other shoe, for the time being, or another. Meanwhile, Chetalee and her foundation have grown wings and taken to the stars.

...

Paying the right price. There's a price to pay for everything in this life, as for the lessons you learn, there's a price for that, too. What one does with those lessons as learned will make a difference in the long run, away from you. Usually, the person who pays to learn the lesson is not always going to be the same one who benefits the most in the long run, I'm guessing. Be sure to pass on what you've learned. Reset any and every system that seeks to remove the elders from the home, and from the lives of the young amongst you, before they're grown. Especially the men, like your male elders, keep them around for as long as you can, if at all you can. So that those young ones don't end up losing out on the lessons of the elders. Don't let them end up having to go back and learn them all over again for themselves, no, not all the time. Because the young ones with no mentors or guides will be repeating past mistakes, be advised. Reliving the experiences of their elders perpetually, and never progressing. Every parent, especially the wise and thinking ones who pay the rent, wants their children to progress. At least a little further than themselves, yes. So, pad it on top of what you've learned, and encourage them to go out and get as much more learning as they can. Then go out and "can" all the learning of the things that they can get. Can it in their minds and their memory. Then rinse out the can and repeat the process down through the ages, so future generations can see how to take a leaf out of your pages. That was how the other man did it; that is how you're going to have to do it, too. Well, what kind of people are we, like you? And, yes, me, too, when we have to depend on the other guy for everything? Like jobs, of course, first and foremost, but that's not all that we depend on others for, for our living. How about food, clothing, and shelter? Don't forget medicine, law, and order. Science, education, even the bare essentials for your... I mean our final dissension. Our final departure is not without a mention, and off to our final destination, the ever-after. For everything, barring none. Say it ain't so. Bring your strong arguments and come, Barrington, let's go.

"Blessings," we say. Yet we beg, steal, and borrow, and don't ever repay. Just hop on the bus and go away, against tomorrow, leaving town for another place, like a complete unknown, and staying "safe."

Who gave you your God's, and the books of rules, supervisory power, and all other tools? The demand for periodic reports, too, is probably designed to keep a watchful eye on you, and me, Boo, every hour. To make sure that what you're doing within your walls conforms to their plans for you and all, probably. Kiss mi damn teeth though, *what a Wolle Heep of an allahbaloo when ebbrey baddy knuoah sei nuttn nuh goh soh.* Much ado about nothing, because everyone already knows that's not the way things usually work and go. But what if a man's seed was an integral part of the survival game, in the grand and glorious schemes of many things, where would this man stand in the game? But we all know that that is not how it goes, so... For that job, you're praying, go out a-searching. But whatever else you may be found doing, remember what I'm saying: robots are coming, and as for them? They ain't praying none.

Black spirituality and religion. Once there were a kind of people, a migratory people who never seemed to have an abiding city. Just like a type of bird that lays its eggs in another bird's nest and moves on. Leaving the hatchlings to be raised by those said other birds in whose nests they were to have dropped off the eggs and moved from, so I've heard. Then those hatchlings would grow up to settle in amongst those of the foster parents' kind and serve them into perpetuity, or until... well, maybe. So, these people will leave and go away. Your people, the very best of your people, I'd say. "An opportunity," they call it, a new job, you say, and mixed it in with the ...it that falls on the grit. But if this is something that happens here every day, like where the best of the rest of you leave and go away? Where does that leave you and me anyway? And you and I, what do we do in this abandoned city? Fight each other over scraps, and about who is pretty, maybe? But what if it should make its way back home, the real truth as to why they had to pick up, pack up, leave, and go out of town. What if the real truth were to be made known to you? Showing up on you, that, what those people did and do, was to make a statement against what you do? They pick up, pack the truck, and leave, going far away from these. Far from you and me and what we do most. "Like, trying to please?"

"Oh, please, yes." That way, they can retain a friendship, too, whenever they happen to come back or while passing through. What if people make a statement with their walking shoes, like, with a tool of mobility, just like you? What if people will vote with their feet, and then stay in the sweet, like, the sweet spot of your good grace? But as for me, I... this wild ass of a guy, I'm going to tell you why I ain't gonna lie. *Look bacca yuh, a nuh ungle di boogie man a cum fei get yuh.* Sorry folks. I tend to get carried away at times with these speeches of spokes and rhymes. You must forgive me, or else. "Else what?"

"Well, for sure, heaven won't be seeing your face for that if you don't, close the door, if nothing else." Fun and jokes aside, though, we as a people need to take a moment to look in the rearview mirror sometimes, to assess and analyze things — "On the clotheslines?"

"Yes, there, even." We need to take periodic looks back over the path we have just come, to see if there are things we could learn. Things to drop off or pick up. Or even if there are things there that are worth holding on to, in the cup, cup... to carry on and continue with. Or we may choose to throw it down and let it sit. Do you think that you have done well? Why then are you so afraid to tell your stories, or have them scrolled and told for you, to your glories...?

"Shut up your mouth," you say, "Don't talk too much, just pray." What is that thing that you're so very afraid of today? That someone might start to talk, perhaps, and then something might slip out from under the tongue where it was parked, start to flap, and a few more folks might get up and start walking away from you and your ah... Could that be it? Of course, if your doings were good and you know it, shouldn't you be itching to tell and show it? Or to have someone else tell and told it, for you? But hold it, what do I know? (Eat). Sheet, boo-boo.

We need to start practicing the art of stock-taking. It may well be because we don't dabble much in the world of business, either. Other than minding other people's business to please her. This may well be why we never seem to take stock of anything but the bin feeder. But we need to, badly. One cannot expect to be doing the same thing constantly, and then be expecting different results, unless — "What, unless it's like coffee?"

"No, unless that one so happens to be... well? You know the rest... of me.

...

The little road that Chii built is now an antique showpiece. His children, too, all his children (no, not you), are now in managerial positions, running not only construction businesses like these into existence. But also: Merchant stores and manufacturing enterprises galore. "Oh, please!"

"Yes, among them, there are also inventors to be found, inventing not only road construction equipment to be put down, but any and every other kind of equipment one might require, as known." Other provinces across China and other places throughout the world are now in construction and upgrade mode. Upgrading the down-the-drain system, too, and the road. Although Chii is now an old man and retired (not to worry), his construction company is still on the job and busy getting hired. Being ably run by a top-class management team, consisting of some of his very own children and grandchildren, wedged somewhere in between. You see where this is going, don't you? Chetalee sure sees it, and that is where she and the foundation are going next, to...

"Start with what you've got," she'd said, "Expect boo-boos along the way. Plan for them, learn from them as you go along, and grow. Strive to be the very best that you can be at whatever it is that you do." Chii's hammer and chisel are in a museum now, preserved for all to come and see, somehow. Come over and see for yourself where it all got started, for him and me under the orchid. Wow!

Like a wise man once said, if you cannot find a job, go create one of your own. You can do that too, or you can go back and sit down. Continue doing what you've been doing, as it is known, like praying for jobs. Luckily for us, though, those things don't happen around our part, only among those other faraway people over there, and afar off. It's time for the wasp to grow up and transition into bees, though. Too much of the stinging and swelling, but not nearly enough of the sweetness of honey to flow, if any, with this bunch of morbidly over-churched people, I'm telling you. Maybe we as a people are cursed and marked for death, though, because we don't "Never seem to get a break," I mean, (ever). Other than for the breaking of the neck, of any, and every one of us who happened to catch a vision for the people, what the heck? Then dared to get up, stand up, and follow after it. Follow up after that vision and see. Look out, Chetalee, they're coming to get you and me. Children of Ham, perhaps, or of a lesser god? "What's this?"

"A piece of spoken word poetry, I think."

Crying, crying, crying over you. I feel like crying, I said, I feel like crying. And you ask me why, Hingh? Well, I can't be lying. It's my people, it is for my people that I'm a-crying. I would have looked, and that's when I would have seen. I saw them there, just across from me, wearing a frown, where there should have been a tear. And yet more tearing down of the gear, of the gown, the garments even. They're angry, mad they are. Righteous indignation burns like hot tar. For all of this nastiness, for the pile of scraps that this traitor has gone and written, there's no forgetting that. No, too, for giving back. But oh, how one would have liked for them to have seen the generous sprinklings of treasures and all other precious things. Scattered unsparingly and growing in between. Which was the only real reason for this, to begin with. The stack of scraps was just there to hide them in. But they are my people, like children, aren't they? This too shall pass on, for this, we'll pray. I must run along now, though, but before I'm done. Of all that's already said, I must remind you of one. The robots are coming, and as for them? They ain't praying none.

Don't worry, though, your breakthrough is on the way. Elkhan, I mean, Akan. Akan has been unmasked and showed up today. You've found him, and his accursed things, you've plucked them out from where they were hiding amongst you. From among them, he has been shown up and cast out; now, look at it, Canaan is in view. Sanctify now yourselves, every one of you; wash your clothes and bathe your skin. Be clean against tomorrow in the evening. Because the bands are coming through, to deliver you, and to take you now over into the lands and into all of the wonderful things that the Lord your God had promised, planned, and had purposed in her heart to do for you, to you. For all of your wonderful people, too. Now, be sure to remain sanctified and holy, even as you are today. Show me, I say, for the Lord your God is holy, and she's coming your way. Never allow another such thing to happen to you. Never allow another such person as Akan to rise, or come in, amongst you, or else, a worse thing than that one might come upon you. Continue now in the right way, as you have made it happen, even to this day. Come, let us now reason together, saith the Lord of the host, and your savior, even God, your father. If no one had told you, you probably would not have known. Because you didn't know it, though, doesn't mean that's not how it went down. So, which of your emotions will rule supreme here today: anger or laughter? Let's choose laughter, I pray; it's medicine to the soul, they say. So, let's laugh at ourselves a little, and maybe we'll begin to live a little bit more on the pickle and love a lot, as before. Yeah! Like that, mi poor... Don't get discouraged by the let-downs and put-downs; use this as fuel for the fire, and you will have arrived home, fully grown-up, higher.

Chapter twenty-four

Cars and Payments.

Suppose with me for a brief moment here. Suppose there was a brother among you, or even a sister, someone who is always talking and telling. Telling all of the wonderful stories of Jeezas, Mister, God, even. She knows all that there is to know about that entity, God. Her god, and how she works and doesn't work. But the sister, or even the brother. Let's stick with the sister here for an even and easy flow from here on, and over the border, if for nothing else, but, hey, lover, let's continue, man. The sister doesn't own a car and has never owned a car. But she is hoping to change that situation soon, that's for sure. She's now learning to drive and has applied for her license. Soon, very soon, she'll be driving too, all over the wild bears and the bison, not you. Just like them, yeah! Just like all of the other blessed, prosperous, and progressive saved people around her, and you, and yes, all of us. Unlike her and Ms. Angus, though, Bro... The brother already owned a car. The brother would have owned several cars in his time. To say that Bro knows cars, or about owning them, is an oxymoron too, to send in on his dime, to spend. But brother doesn't know nearly as much as Sis. about the "God business and the bits," "No?" "No, not that much about the godly siding," surely not enough for him to join the choir and sing. Well, not yet. He will soon know, though. That same sister and other sweet whisperers are seeing about that row. Sis doesn't miss out on a chance at schooling the brother on the things of God, which, she surely knows an awful lot about, if nothing else. And who is Bro to argue with her on these subject matters? Bro won't, because if there is one other thing that Bro knows a thing or two about, two counts? Bro knows that he can't win there without... You know, like, without much luck. But it was to come upon a memorable day that Sis would have gotten into another bit of her usual telling of things to say in talks, like this. Telling tales of what is and what isn't, and yet more telling tales of what is going to be in fact. She's going to be the proud owner of a car, not me, soon. Bravo to the sister, and congratulations to you, Sis. But you know, Sis, that little miss! Sis is not going to stop until you and I know every single detail. As well as the ins and outs of the whole thing, now on resale. So, on and on she went, telling and tolling until the story was almost told when...

Almost because she was to be stopped abruptly in the middle of the telling tracks, and cause of the cars too. That would have happened when the brother had to do some telling of his own, as in the talk queue. Sister had gotten to the point where she was lamenting the car payments on the loans. Bro had to tell her that she doesn't have to have any of those to overcome, not a red cent, to pose. Now, sing-along; no, not one, no, not one.

"What? Car payments?"

"Yes, car payments."

Surprised she was to be, or was she? Not if arguing on issues that Sis knows all of the knowing on, were any indication as to who gets the final word on an issue going on; any issue. This was not going to be any different for the missis; that was for sure a thing, for the misuse. She knows a lot of things, and if there is anything she knows well? She surely knows that; if you have a car, you have also got car payments to make for...

"Like, for the license, registration, plate, insurance, and such, the likes of a street race, right?"

"No, like monthly payments, for the car. That's what people do, no? People who own cars, no?"

"Are you asking? Or telling me?"

"I'm telling you, everybody I know who has cars has car payments to make."

"I have a car; I have owned several cars in my time, some of them carried payments for a while, yes, but not all. I don't have car payments on my current car; I bought and paid for it, with cash." Pick up her jaw off the floor for me, will you? and fast. So, the schooler is now about to be schooled on the only thing in the world that she didn't know, seemingly. Or is it so, like, feeling me? Now go, Willie Nilly. You have a car payment, Miss, because you wanted to be driving a car. Just like you have been seeing other people doing, like the Joneses, for instance, and Sue Hingh, with her. But you don't have the money to pay for it, just like some other people in the world do and did. Many people do that when buying cars and shoes, and roasting parts from pigs. But that's not all. Not all of them do bottled booze on the gigs; some prefer to do her in bars, not just as it applies to cars, as these things are. But most other big-ticket items and things, those that those other people of the world would buy and cringe at. They made sure that they knew where the money would be coming from to pay for it, though, even before they went shopping and bought all kinds of sheets, no?

"No, stop it."

But there are some other people in the world, too, some from among the previously mentioned bunch, no, not you. Those who know how to get other people's money to come to them continuously. People's money, like yours, and yes, mine too, sometimes, Ms. Lee. So, they provide you, I mean, "us," with the money you will need to go out and buy things you don't need, so funny. *Cuss.* For five, nine, twenty-nine times the cost. Then, they'll have you paying them back over a long period, and at high interest rates, on top of that. None of which you saw at any point in the bargaining session, swap. No, not at any time at all, since you weren't looking back, like, at such things, ever, and even to a fall. Like you never bothered to do; look at anything, that's who. You would have called it all a blessing. Confessing about how the Lord had blessed you with a new car, and thing, and Ting. But not many days later, the bank came in and repossessed the "blessing" with which the Lord had once blessed... sorry, I meant to say, the car. The bank would have repossessed the car. You buy the house next, more blessings, you boast, but the bank is threatening to take that too, the blessing with which the Lord once blessed you, we'd supposed. Meanwhile, the brother would have seen and heard enough; the "Doubt seeds" were starting to breed up again, from the dust. So, whereas Bro was skeptical long ago, wondering about some things he had seen and heard, being ascribed to the wonderful, marvelous doings and sayings of the Lord, and wanting so very much to believe it is true. So that he may know that there's something higher and greater than him and you; the brother was a-searching and believing, and a-working, and praying. Peradventure, there was some truth to what they were saying, in what he was to be heard coming out of them, and daring. Like, that one day the Lord would wake up from her slumber and start the business of governing her kingdom. Just like she once did and got it done, and like she will again do, in times to come, as reported by many and yet more "some." But she would not come, and Bro's faith starts to wane some... Maybe she will one day come or go. Or do something else that will be able to show proof to the naysayers that she really and truly is in command. Are we worshiping a God that's wrong? Tell me, which one? Well, after this encounter with the sister, the very sister in whom the brother had placed much faith, Mister. At least, he had placed a lot of faith in her sayings to date, and her many testimonies of faith. Because Bro didn't know those things for sure, the things of which she had spoken on ends, from both sides of the flip-flopping door frame. But Bro had long harbored some doubt, a somewhat healthy dose of godly doubt. Now, though, Brother's doubt has been multiplied, just like all the incidents of people who had told him lies. Or tell him things he'd found hard to swallow, and now, bro is thinking of stopping from follow... But before he does and makes a mistake, Bro decides to throw them a bait, and then wait. What they choose to do in response will decide the matter once and for all. They would have picked it up, and sure was the fall, they swallowed the bait, hook, line, sinker, and all. Wrong call, boss, your loss.

Now, tell me, did the brother do wrong or right, as you see it in your informed vision and spiritual sight? Wouldn't you have done the very same if you were to be found caught up in such a game? But then again. What if you already are, like, caught up? No, not into heaven but up anyway, as in, a game to play? Don't you think it is time now for us to start thinking about these and other such things? Just a few more things to throw into the mixing tin with Justin, whenever you get started at doing the stinking thinking sin ting on tough skin. What if you had struck the rock, though, when you were only supposed to have spoken, slow, like, really slow, Leigh, perhaps? Now, this, not that.

One guy sees money as a tool. He uses it to take in lots more of the same money and to buy valuable things for his household name, not to be funny. The other guy, though, sees money as a fool. Just something to go out and spend, buying expensive rubbish, and swimming pools. Which ends up in the landfill again, and very quickly so. What if a tiny portion of the world's population is out there busily manipulating things, like gathering all the wealth and the resources unto themselves, from him, while playing the swan song for others to sing? Like luring the many others along, like you and me, the unsuspecting ones to see. Luring us down to the ultimate doom, another pile of balloons, right? Nice. Speaking of nice, sing along with me now: been so nice to be with you, so very nice, but...

Chapter twenty-five

Just a Bit More: What-ifs.
What if the banks are actively manipulating things to disadvantage the disenfranchised, unsuspecting clients even further?

"Rubbish?"

What if the Elk had seen and heard of it before?

"More rubbish?"

Here, though, is a scenario, just for you, oh, and yours... Go.

The Elk was privy to a situation where his classmate and friend almost lost his house, just at the point where he was starting to look forward to retirement and staying the course. The house was pretty much paid up for by then, of course. Whatever payments he has left to make from this point on will be more than manageable for him to carry on. He didn't think he had to pay super close attention to the mortgage account and the repayment amounts. He just needed to continue doing what he has always been doing, as he has always done with an "Amen." He'll be okay, right, with the Lord's help and all, tonight? "Wrong."

It so happened that, over time, he would have noticed that there was quite a bit of money in his bank account and growing. Meanwhile, the rickety old car was getting "*Ricketier*" by the day and slowing. Old friend-a-mine is going to have to do something about the car soon, and that was just what my old friend did, before noon. He went out and bought himself a new car, well, not so much new that far, let's just say, another car, to stay on the safe side, where you are. A fine piece of machinery it was indeed. Finer even than you are, Ingrid, just kidding, yes indeed. After all, my old friend was headed into retirement; it would be nice to arrive there in style, he meant, wouldn't it be? Needless to say, my old friend was staring down some real trouble not many days later, on the driveway near the crater, at home where he prays at the altar behind his gate, Sir. Of course, he didn't have the kind of money to buy that kind of car. "How is that possible?" you'd asked away, at her. I'll tell you how, anyway. When you or anyone else is the type of person my old friend has been all his life. The type who has humongous faith in God and miracles in the skies, whether or not there was any real evidence of such things ever working out in his favor, to go by and eyes... Be it in his past, in his vehicles, or in his electric shaver, guys. When one has spent a lifetime waiting for that miracle to show up and save her, it likely will. It will show up. Whether or not it is God-sent or man-made, a miracle will show up for him to go and save. So, what if this person was, at the time, praying for a new car? Which, by all accounts and indications, he probably was, as you are. The current car was running on a prayer, and prayer only. He was praying for another to come in and get homely. Then, all of a sudden, he began to notice that money was (seemingly) miraculously building up in his bank account, and fast approaching the exact amount that he needed to get him the car of his dreams, mi Count. What if he had by then settled himself securely in the idea that God does work like that? In mysterious ways, even, and that it was, in fact, her (or his...) No, not Sister Eden, but her, his Godly friend. Yes, it was his God who sent him the money, as it occurred. What if he then went out on a buying date and purchased the car he so much wanted to take? Then went to church, testifying about how the Lord had blessed him again and given him the new car he had wanted and had been praying for, for many days on end. What if, not many days later, the sad realization was to come home to him on the wager, that it was, in fact, the house money? It was the mortgage payments that the bank had stopped taking on the regular schedule as before was the case, for whatever reason. What if the reason was the same as it was in the Elk's case, where they had said that the mortgage was not renewed, so they stopped collecting the payments? Real smooth. Even though they had never done it that way before, to him. Even under said types of situations, with an amen, and then again. What if they have a habit of doing such things to some very select types of clients? Clients who portray certain profile traits like these are, in my hands, where they cannot seem to be able to get their hands on emergency funds to save their own lives unless it's to save their lives. What if the banks were to then set out to create such a "convenient" emergency? What if they had noticed a pattern where this, as well as other such types of clients, has a history of running out and spending every extra penny that may become available to them, like science, real or imagined? Their own or borrowed money? What if they had noticed that this particular client was ripe and ready for a big-ticket item, such as a new car, for instance, to ride in? They couldn't have known that, though, because they don't have that sort of information on file, and they sure can't get it by just dialing up a number to call. Nor by hitting the link up against the wall, right? "Wrong, they sure can." What if the bank sees this as an opportunity? What if the banks were in the habit of creating opportunities? Such sorts of "opportunities even for themselves, and for their friend Steven, from where none seemed to exist before that very evening, on the shelf?" Good evening, Michelle, my belle. What if they were in the business of making money, lots of money, for as long as they can and from whomever they can? But then again, this is a moot point because we all know that that is not how it goes. Mutant Pinochet, "under your nose," now this is where you should drop in and say; Right. "Right." But... okay, let's get back to doing this to the finish tonight. What if they also have other suggestive tools and tactics? What if it were one such suggestive tool that they had used when they had cut the insurance on the brother's mortgage? Suggesting that the brother could consider this option, too, should things get a bit tough on the cartridge for him and you? They already have all the evidence that they would need right there at their fingertips under the reed, enough to know that things will get tougher with the brother, no? If that wasn't the case, they have also got the ways and means to make it all happen, some way or the other? "So?" What if that was the very reason why they were so aggressive in getting that particular question answered every time? Like, when they'd called up the brother about the unresolved mortgage issue, and the prime... rates? What if not having insurance on the house and hence, on the mortgage, is the quickest and easiest way to get legal and innovative and start the moves to take everything away from the brother, in the ordeals, the same as you and every other? What if that was the very next thing that they were about to do when they had said, "If there's no insurance on the house, Sir, the bank will take legal action?" Not May, but Will. What if one were to survey these types of everyday people who have mortgage issues with their financial institutions? What is the likelihood that they would have had similar experiences as this once or twice, but keep it to themselves, thinking that they are the only ones who are wise? They're the only ones who are experiencing such issues with their banks. What's that? What if none of this is a Hypothesis? Am I still allowed to ask about this? I hope I am.

Meanwhile, though, the old man has been sitting there and watching. Hearing, listening, seeing, explaining, giving, forgiving, and writing. Amongst other things, to ride in. Hear him, because...

Some savage beasts from a wilderness theme. Again, bit the brother hard in the crust of his bloodstream, for pain. Oh, how he cried out, oh how the brother screamed, but no one was found worthy to reach out and save him, or so, to some, it would have seemed. He had to holler out, yet the more, had to curse, just to stop himself from popping open, blowing up, kaboom, and bursting at the bore. Could he find you doing the wrong thing, though, when upon his imminent return, if he should find you and me, like, drifting, drifting away? Like you've been seen doing, every day, even while they are doing all of those other things. Like, while you were there, lean... lean, leaning? Leaning on the wrong side of everything? Of course, not you, only the other Hugh, I mean, the other Ewe, as in the Elk, yes, him, as it is in this case, and the washbasin. He's the only one who could be found guilty of such chased things. *But choh man, shut up yuh mouth nuh. Yuh chat too much already.* And then, look, look at him go.

Chapter twenty-six

Who's Watching the Old Man?
The Elk was about to meet up with the old man for the first time, again. It was cold out, but he needed a workout. He put on his jogging shoes, then put the cap upon his head, pulled it up and over you, no?

"No, just over the head."

"OH!" Look, he pulled over the hoodie too, then bounced off into the crisp morning air.

Meanwhile, look. Look at this, over on this side here, the old man is sitting in a chair. It's almost freezing there in the old rocking chair. The disdain he's showing for the frigid fall air. He's still listening and hearing things, thinking and talking to himself, even. Talking about nothing, it would seem. Good evening. Nothing but...

The Elk is approaching the peripheries of the old man's housing; he'd looked up and seen him. Now look, his strides are shortening and slowing, down to just a jog and... almost a walk now. Because — "What, because he owes him something and doesn't want to, to...?"

"No, well..." nothing. The old man saw him coming, running, as he was to be seen coming in. His breathing was heavy as he approached. The head, or more like the hoodie covering the head, was bobbing... running some more now as he goes, no, more like, come. He's coming on up and getting closer to the old man. His head is still bobbing to and from as it grows taller and clearer to him, coming over the steep up-hill climb. Look, he's just about walking now. Elk was panting hard and

breathing rather heavily as he watched the hilltop draw near and hence...
"Oh, Lord." The relief is felt now, for the downside and a much easier
workload, from going with the wind. He's running much more than be-
fore now. No, He's not jogging anymore, wow.

But then, that was when he would have looked and seen him there,
the old man, sitting in the rocking chair and doing more of the nothings
that he was known to be doing, with his own hands, always. Only by
those who knew him, though, not so much the Elk; he didn't know him
that well. Other than for that time when he would have looked up and
seen him sitting there, as he was soon to be passing by the old man's
chair. Running.

And he, the old man, would have been there thinking and talking
to himself, like always. The old man is there again today, writing. He's
always writing things down in a book, the right thing. In a journal or
something, anything that can be eternal, or to go with dumplings when
he cooks, the kernel, other than for that, look.

The Elk now cuts the speed of the running a bit. Slowly, he's rolling,
as he gets closer to him, yes, to where the old man sits, there. Then he
cuts it down to a walk, what? Look at that. Now he's standing, no, not
quite, but bending forward, hunched with both hands on the knee up-
front and panting. Oh, Lord! He's breathing as hard as if it were a wind
fan that would have hit him up against the planting. Straightening up
again. Just standing there now with both hands akimbo and looking,
looking at the old man there, doing nothing, other than those things
that he's always known to be doing. Like, much more, nothing.

Walking off now, and then stopping, again, and staring at him, yes,
at the old man who was sitting, still. And he, the old man! Look, he just
picked up the coffee cup. Now he's sipping on the cup, the old man is
sipping on the coffee cup and staring over the brim at the looker man
looking at him.

Walking again, Elk is walking away slowly, and looking back at him,
yes, at the old man, not me. The old man is taking a break from drink-
ing, tea, or savoring the coffee and thinking of me, well, probably. But

certainly, from talking to himself and writing, he's now just staring back at him, pardon me, not you. It's his coffee break, he can do whatever he wants and for as long as he wants to date... He's slowly rolling the cup now in the palm of his hands; wait... "Roll on slowly, mister man." Now he's talking to himself, again, in a hushed tone, and rolling the cup, round and round still.

The Elk runs off and speeds it up a little; he's now slowing down to do something in the middle, and stopping, again. He's turning around, look, he just turned around, to look back at the old man who's still sitting down. He is still there talking; the old man is talking to himself. But the Elk, look, he just looked up, what is he...

"Will you shut the cup up?" he swore at the old man, who didn't answer back but looked up at him some more. He did not respond; the old man just reached up with a confident right hand, grabbed and stroked a handful of white beards. Thinking, think, and thinking some more, but look here.

Out in the distance, look at that, there he goes, the Elk is going, up the road, not so slowly anymore, but... going.

The old man is writing, writing again... Going.

And thinking his thoughts in colorful languages... Going.

Of some things that he would like to say to him, there he is... Going.

Seeing faces in beautiful shades... Going still. And plain green pastures out on the glades... Going.

Look, he now put away the pen and the writing pad... Going.

Or was it a journal that he had? Anyway, the Elk is still... Going.

The old man gets up, turns around, and walks towards the front door to close it down... Growing smaller as he's... Going.

The old man stepped inside, turned, and was about to close the door behind him, but not before looking up once more at him... Going, what little is left of him, going.

The old man tugged his nose and pouted at him just before... look. He's gone. The old man finishes closing the door at home. It's way past his bedtime now, he's beat, he's spent, all used up, one might say, the old man is, altogether. Done.

The End.

"Note from the author." Just a note of thanks to you for choosing to read my book and for sticking with the story, even to the end. You must have liked it an awful lot. At this point, I want to thank you very much for your patronage, and I also ask you, my reader, to take a minute or two to post a review of the book on the Sales pages at Amazon and any other such sales pages, or wherever you bought it. This small gesture is so very important to us and very much appreciated. Don't keep it to yourself; be sure to share this. Thank you.

Special thanks to these people who have helped in various ways in bringing about this book. To my immediate as well as the extended family: To Leonie and Charles, who had to put up with me not being quite there at times, even when I might have been there in the body. In the end, your support was unwavering and unmistakable. Thank you. To my friends and extended family who supported me by allowing me the time and space, and also physically, by spending your hard-earned cash with me, to purchase the books, or by telling others about them. Thank you.

So why do I write? I hear you ask.

The answer is this: I'm a guy of many words, but whose tongue is slow and heavy, and my words tend to come out awkward and clumsy, so I write because I always have something to say, even when no one will listen. I think. Which always tends to get me into trouble anyway. The bonus, though, in writing is that a pencil usually comes with an eraser. The Writingelk

E Lloyd Kelly is WritingElk, an Author, poet, and blogger. Born in Jamaica West Indies, to Raglan and Alma Kelly. Now resides in Montreal Quebec.

Other works by E Lloyd Kelly, includes:

How to train a wild puppy dog named, Manley,

The "REAL INKY TRAIL" book series

Aloada's Shirt Factory

Collect Call. Among others

Find these and others on the Author's page at Amazon.com/author/elloydkelly   https://www.amazon.com/E.-Lloyd-Kelly/e/B01G7NYWL6

www.ingramcontent.com/pod-product-compliance
Lightning Source LLC
Chambersburg PA
CBHW061149120626
46546CB00005B/1992